THE HARD MAN

The
Hard Man

A PLAY BY

TOM McGRATH
and
JIMMY BOYLE

EDINBURGH

CANONGATE

1977

CANONGATE PUBLISHING LTD
17 *Jeffrey Street, Edinburgh* EH1 1DR

First published Edinburgh 1977.

Hardback 0-903937-57-3
Paperback 0-903937-53-0

Printed in Great Britain
by LINDSAY & CO. LTD.,
17 *Blackfriars Street, Edinburgh.*

THE HARD MAN *was first performed at the Traverse Theatre Club, Edinburgh, on* 19 *May* 1977, *with the following cast:*

MARTIN BLACK	Slugger, Renfrew
MIKE CARTER	Deadeye, Archie, Kelley, Policeman, Clerk of Court, Mochan
IAN IRELAND	Big Danny, Policeman, Lewis the Lawyer, Commando, Paisley
PETER KELLY	Byrne
FRANCIS LOW	Lizzie, Carole, Woman's voice
ANN SCOTT-JONES	Maggie, Maw, Woman (who's with Archie), Barwoman, Didi
BENNY YOUNG	Bandit, Johnstone
RONNIE GOODMAN	Percussionist

Directed by PETER LICHTENFELS
Designed by BOB LAST
Lighting by ALASTAIR McARTHUR

ACT ONE

Lights come down. Darkness. Fragment of a song:

SONG   *Oh the River Clyde's a wonderful sight,*
the name of it thrills me and fills me with pride.
Oh I'm satisfied whate'er may betide,
the Sweetest of Songs is the Song of the Clyde.

*Lights come up on The Windae-hingers—two women, LIZZIE and
MAGGIE, leaning out of their tenement house windows. They have
their elbows on the window-ledge and are having a conversation
across the street.*

LIZZIE   Hullo, Maggie.

MAGGIE   Hullo there, Lizzie.

LIZZIE   Maggie, where did your man come frae?

MAGGIE   Seymour Street. Ah hear its getting awfae bad up there. Ah
think we just moved oot in time.

LIZZIE   Yir no kiddin. Thir wus a man kilt up thair the other night. The
Spaniard. Did you know him?

MAGGIE   Oh aye. McTaggart the Mad Spaniard. Everybody knew him.
He wus a right bad loat. Ah might've known he'd come tae a sticky
end. Whit happened tae him enyway?

LIZZIE   He wus laying oan the street in Maryhill Road—just ootside
the HLI pub fur oors an' oors. We wur oan the buses, oan the
night-service, an' we saw him laying there up an' doon fur aboot four
journies. Even from the bus in the dark you could see the blood. They
say they put the knife in at the bottom of his stomach and ripped him
open.

MAGGIE   Did the polis no dae anythin aboot it?

LIZZIE   Naw. Thae jist let him lie thair. They wur glad tae be rid o him.

MAGGIE   And did they no get anyone fur it?

LIZZIE   They never dae in gang fights, dae they? Oh but see efterwards,
when they took the body away, we passed back doon oan the bus an

7

aw you could see wus the chalk marks and the blood. And the Spaniard wusnae thair anymair . . .

Lights down. Windae-hingers withdraw.

BYRNE, SLUGGER *and* BANDIT *rush on the stage in a state of alarm, looking behind them. They are obviously being pursued.* BYRNE *is alert but not afraid. They have stopped for a moment, breathless, looking back.*

BANDIT   Oh my God! Oh . . . my . . . God!

BYRNE   *Annoyed* Whit's the matter wae yae?

BANDIT   Whit dae you think?

SLUGGER   Aye. Naebody sed enythin aboot fuckin murder . . .

BYRNE   Ah didnae touch that mug.

BANDIT   No half yae didnae!

BYRNE   Listen, Bandit. You were in another room when it happened— enjoying the party—you never saw nothing. Same goes fur you, Slugger. You saw nothing neither. That mob will try tae put the finger oan me fur it, but ah didnae touch him. Huv you goat me?

SLUGGER   Goat yae.

BANDIT   *More reluctantly* Goat yae.

BYRNE   *Smiling, extending his open palm* Right! Put it there, chinas! We're aw in it thegither! *They both slap his outstretched palm with their hands and say their line.*

BANDIT   *Slapping* We're aw in it thegither!

SLUGGER   *Slapping* We're aw in it thegither!

BYRNE   O.K. Lets scarper. Different directions.

SLUGGER   See you doon the boozer.

BYRNE   Aye, in aboot an oor's time. But go tae the other boozer, no the usual wan. They'll be looking fur us there . . .

Exit BANDIT *and* SLUGGER. *Light change.* BYRNE *steps forward, looking around the audience.*

My name is Byrne. Johnnie Byrne. I was born in the Gorbals District of Glasgow. You've read about me in the newspapers and heard about me in pubs. I'm a lunatic. A right bad lot. What the Judge always calls, "A menace to society". I'm speaking to you tonight from a Scottish prison where I am serving life-sentence for murder. What you are going to see is my life as I remember it. What you are going to hear is my version of the story.

SLUGGER *and* BANDIT *run on shouting.*

SLUGGER   Rats.

BANDIT   Chasin' rats.

SLUGGER   Chasin' rats roon the backs.

BANDIT   Chasin' rats roon the backs wae a wee dug . . .

SLUGGER   Chasin' rats roon the backs wae a wee dug that wus rerr ut brekkin their necks.

BANDIT   It even goat a mention in the papers that wee dug, because it kilt that many rats.

SLUGGER   Hiya, Johnny.

BYRNE   Hiya, Slugger. Hiya, Bandit. Back tae school again . . . *This line by way of explanation to audience.*

SLUGGER   School! School! Back tae school. Ah hate a Monday.

BANDIT   Ah hate the fuckin' school. School's rubbish!

SLUGGER   Aye, whit's it aw aboot anyway? Who wants to learn aw that shite they teach yae?

BYRNE   You're that stupit, yae couldnae learn anythin anyway, even if yae wahntit tae.

SLUGGER   Listen to who's talkin. The teacher says you're a dead cert fur truble. He's goat you marked doon fur the Borstal already.

BYRNE   Fuck 'im.

BANDIT   Fancy doggin' it?

SLUGGER   Aye. Fancy it? We could go doon the shoaps an' dae some knockin'. Fancy it, Johnny?

BYRNE   Och, I don't know. We did that yesterday—and the day before. Ah think we're just wastin' oor time. Bars a chocolate an' boatles o scoosh. Ah wis aboot sick yesterday wae the amount ah ate.

BANDIT   Well, you were the wan that insistit oan goin' back tae the shoap an daein' it agen.

BYRNE   That wis just because ah wus bored. There's no much fun tae it wance you've done it a few times. An' enyway, its no bars o choclate we need, its money!

SLUGGER   Back tae that agen.

9

BANDIT   You bet your life its back tae that. Money. Lolly. Cash. It aw comes back tae that sooner or later, doesn't it?

BYRNE   Aye, well you know how we were talkin aboot daein a few shoaps at night?

BOTH   Aye.

BYRNE   An' we were tryin tae figure oot how we wid dae the loaks?

BOTH   Aye.

BYRNE   Well, I've been thinking . . .

BOTH   Miracles!

BYRNE   During the day, when they close up the shop for a coupla hours tae go hame an' huv a bit tae eat an' a wee snooze, maybe a pint doon ut the boozers . . . they cannae be bothered pittin aw thae loaks oan . . . its no worth it fur the shoart time thair oot . . . and enyway, they know that thieves only wurk ut night . . .

He smiles at them. They think about this.

. . . so . . . if we go during the day . . .

SLUGGER   Goat ye.

BANDIT   Ya beauty.

BYRNE   So whit ur we waitin fur? Cumoan.

To audience.

I can't tell you about my chromosomes or genetic structure and I can't say anything about my Oedipus Complex or my Ego and my Id. Battered babies grow up to be people who batter babies. But I got nothing but affection when I was young—from my mother. My father—sometimes we wouldn't see him for days on end then he'd come home triumphant wae presents for everybody and half-bottle of whisky in his back pocket.

One night he came home, lifted me up to the window, and said—"Look down there, son. What do you see?" I saw a brand new, shining motorcar. "It's all yours", he said. "Tomorrow we'll go fur a hurl in it." The next day I got up and looked out of the window. But the car was gone. And so was my father. And I never saw him again.

I remember my brothers and I at the funeral. There were four of us and we were sitting round the coffin, giggling. We wouldn't have laughed if we'd known what was coming.

SLUGGER *and* BANDIT *run on, pretending to be kids in the street teasing* BYRNE.

10

SLUGGER   Poorhoose! Poorhoose!

BANDIT   Look ut the Byrnes wae thir big broon suits an their tackety boots. Poorhoose! Poorhoose!

BYRNE   Him an' his brothers sleep four tae a bed!

BANDIT   Poorhoose! Poorhoose!

SLUGGER   *He and* BANDIT *are exiting as* MOTHER *enters.* Their mammy's a skivvy fur the West End toafs.

BOTH   *Exiting* Poorhoose! Poorhoose!

BYRNE *and his* MOTHER

BYRNE   Hey Maw. Gonnae lend me half a knicker?

MAY   How? Where are you goin?

BYRNE   Ah'm goin oot wae the boys.

MAW   Where ti? Ah hope you're no going galavantin aw o'er the place and gettin intae trouble an' hiven the polis up at this door?

BYRNE   Ah'm no goin anywhere. Ah just want the money fur the pictures.

MAW   Ah've no goat that much. Here's a dollar, that'll huv tae dae yi. Be in here sharp the night. Ah've tae get up at five the morn.

BYRNE   You know ah'm always in early, Maw.

MAW   Aye. That'll be right. Aw ah know is yir always bringin the polis tae the door and givin that auld nosey bastard across the road somethin' tae talk about.

BYRNE   Don't worry aboot hur, Maw. She's been gossipping oot hur windae so long she's left hur diddie-marks oan the windae sill.

Exit BYRNE

MAW   Right you. That's enough. Watch yir tongue. Mind and be in here early and nae fighting nor cerryin oan. *To audience.* Och, he wusnae a bad boy really. It wus the company he kept. Ah could never believe aw the bad things people said aboot him, no even after he went tae prison. He wus ma son and he wus never any boather tae me. Ah mean, whit chance did he huv? He went alang tae the youth club an him an his mates were barred the very first night. Troublemakers! They were the very wans that needed some help. When he was younger, he wantit tae be an altar boy. But he wusnae allowed because he didnae huv any sandshoes—and ah couldnae afford tae buy him any. It wus oanly the toaffs that could afford tae kneel oan God's altar. Of course, toaffs tae us wur the people that lived jist up the street. In those days the television wus a new thing and it wus a great

11

sign of wealth if yae hud a telly. We wur lucky if we hud enough tae keep us in food from day to day, nae wonder the boy turned tae thievin. He used tae come home wae presents fur me—things fur the hoose an' sometimes even a bit of money—and he'd pretend he'd worked fur thaim. Ah knew how he'd come by them and ah didnae like it and sometimes ah wid refuse his gifts. But maist o the time ah accepted—ah hud no option.

SLUGGER *and* BANDIT *run on to the stage.* MAW *exits behind them.*

SLUGGER   Nylons.
BANDIT   Bevvy.
SLUGGER   Trannies.
BANDIT   Dresses. We supplied the loat.
SLUGGER   The people couldnae afford tae buy things frae the shoaps—
BANDIT   It was a social service. *Pointing to himself* To our society at any rate. It aw depends which side o the fence yir oan, doesn't it? Presents fur Christmas, a boatle fur Ne'erday, the orders wur always placed wae us. And Johnny Byrne became a popular young man about the Gorbals—a contact much sought after.
SLUGGER   While we made a foartune. Well, no much o a fortune but enough to keep us going for a while. For, after all, we were growing boys . . .

Enter DEADEYE *and* BYRNE *from opposite sides of the stage. They walk straight into next scene which includes* BANDIT *and* SLUGGER. DEADEYE *speaks through his nose.*

DEADEYE   Hello there, Johnny. Hiya, boys.
BOYS   *Together* Hiya, Deadeye!
They do this greeting in style but DEADEYE *is intent on his business with* BYRNE. *He is a small man in his forties. He goes straight to the point.*
DEADEYE   Listen, Johnny, ah blagged some shirts there. Dae yae want tae buy any?
BYRNE   Let me see whit like they ur.
DEADEYE   Look at that. The best o' swag, Johnny, an' thair a real bargain so they urr.
BYRNE   How many huv yae goat?
DEADEYE   A gross. And ah'm puntin thaim cheap at a knicker each.

12

BYRNE Och, cumon, Deadeye. Yir no trying tae punt thaim tae me at that price.

DEADEYE Whit dae yae want? Dae yae want me tae throw thaim away? Ye'll no get shurts like that in the shoaps fur under a fiver.

BYRNE Ah tell yae what, Deadeye. I'll give you half a knicker each fur thaim an' ...

DEADEYE Naw, naw ...

BYRNE ... an' ah'll take the loat.

DEADEYE The loat? A hale gross. You wid never get rid o them.

BYRNE Let me worry aboot that. You take care o your end and ah'll take care of mine. Where ur the shurts? Doon ut the hoose? Right, Slugger, you go wae the wee yin an' pick up the rest o thaim. Ah'll settle up wae yae later, Deadeye.

Exit DEADEYE *and* SLUGGER. SLUGGER *gently persuading* DEADEYE *on his way,* DEADEYE *a bit bemused by it all.*

You take these doon tae Isaac the tailor and tell him he cun huv a groass o thaim ut Thirty Boab each.

BANDIT Right-oh, Johnny.

Takes shirts and exits. BYRNE *left alone on stage.*

BYRNE So we'd progressed. We'd started at the age of five, going round the doors collecting firewood and empty bottles, it was only a tiny step to stealing bars of chocolate, and a tiny step further to breaking locks and squeezing through windows. By this time I'd already done an Approved School stretch—for breaking into bubble gum machines, and I was beginning to get a sense of the way things are stacked. I cried my eyes out the night they took me away, pleaded with them and promised I would never do it again—it had only been a joke and I didn't feel I had done anything wrong but it was too late—

SLUGGER *and* BANDIT *have re-entered.*

SLUGGER Alright, Byrne, stop dreaming. Strip. Wash. Scrub this in your hair, you little heap of vermin—grab hold of that bucket and SCRUB THAT FLOOR!

BYRNE But I scrubbed it yesterday and the day before.

SLUGGER Well, scrub it again.

BANDIT And don't but me, sonny, you're going to have to learn!

SLUGGER That floor has been scrubbed a thousand times by boys like you down the years, and it'll be scrubbed a thousand times more, because, you know, its not the scrubbing that counts, not the sparkle off the floor, no its the lesson you learn while you're scrubbing.

BANDIT   And do you know what that is, Byrne? Or dae yae want us tae tell yae?

SLUGGER   Respect! Respect fur authority!

BANDIT   That's right. Respect fur authority. Authority. *Brandishes cane* Authority.

They are circling him, threateningly. BANDIT *has a cane. He becomes increasingly aroused.*

SLUGGER   Authority and Private Property. *Irish accent. Mimics priest. Makes blessing in the air* Blessed be Private Property Now and Forever Amen.

BANDIT   *Almost diabolic. Thrashing with the cane in rhythm to the words.*
Whack Whack Whack
On Your Bare Backside.
Just to make sure
You Don't Try it Again.

Gives a final whack and stands back. Breathless. Wipes his brow. SLUGGER *takes on a mock air of schoolteacher. Produces a tawse from within his jacket and flexes it.* BYRNE *remains cowering back, his hands up to protect himself.* SLUGGER *speaks straight to the audience.*

SLUGGER   Personally I prefer the tawse to the cane—flesh against flesh, it seems more humane.

BYRNE *stands up slowly, with the bucket in his hand, carefully considering* SLUGGER *who is giving the audience a demonstration of how to use the tawse.* BYRNE *lifts the bucket and empties it over* SLUGGER'S *head. Slow blackout on* SLUGGER *dancing in rage with bucket on his head—*BYRNE *and* BANDIT *doubled up, laughing.*

Lights come back up on the Windae-hingers, MAGGIE *and* LIZZIE

MAGGIE   Howurr things, Lizzie?

LIZZIE   No bad. They could be better. Ma back's killin me an that doctoar doon the street's nae use at aw.

14

MAGGIE   Aye. Ah've changed away frae him. No so much because o him but o that bitch that cleans his office. Just because she writes oot his prescriptions fur him, she thinks she's a nurse.

LIZZIE   Aye, she bloody annoys me so she does, the way she struts aboot that surgery like the Queen o Sheba an' hur wae hur hoose like a midden an thae weans o hurs in a terrible state. She ought tae be ashamed o hursel.

MAGGIE   She hud the cheek tae tap a shilling aff o me fur the meter an ah huvnae seen her since. Ah'll be needin it back by Friday tae—ah need every penny!

LIZZIE   Ah'm in the same boat. Ah've goat the man comin in tae empty the meter this afternoon because ah need the rebate. Ah've nae money tae get the tea in fur him comin hame fae work.

MAGGIE   Ah'm expecting that H.P. man. Ah canna pay him this week an ah owe him six weeks awready.

LIZZIE   If ah see him comin ah'll send wan o the weans up tae shout through the letter box.

MAGGIE   Aye and let me know when he goes away cos the old bastard always stauns wae his ear ti the door listenin fur me . . .

They both withdraw. Enter BYRNE, SLUGGER *and* BANDIT. *Rock beat from percussionist.*

BANDIT   Johnny, the lads up in Shamrock Street wahnt us tae go o'er thair an' gie them haunders. There's a team comin doon frae the Calton tae dae them over.

BYRNE   We're a thievin gang. We're no a fightin gang like thaim.

BANDIT   But they're just the next street, Johnny.

SLUGGER   Aye, and if we don't dae it, they'll say we crapped it.

BYRNE *thinks it over.*

BYRNE   Is there weapons?

BANDIT   That Calton team will huv bayonets and chains, boatles—the lot.

BYRNE   We better arm oorsels tae then.

BANDIT   Ah've goat a blade stashed away in the hoose.

SLUGGER   Wait till yae see the chib ah've goat. You'll never believe it.

15

SLUGGER *and* BANDIT *stage a mock fight behind* BYRNE *as he speaks to audience. They have weapons and they stalk one another, leap on one another pretending to stab and hit.*

BYRNE   Blades. Hammers. A splinter of glass. Anything did—just so long as it made a mark. A new dimension had entered my life. A new reality had opened up for me. Violence. It was inevitable. Sometimes violence has a reason on the streets—its political, or religious, or a junkie killing for drugs—either a reason or an excuse. But in the world that I come from, violence is its own reason. Violence is an art form practised in and for itself. And you soon get to know your audience and what it is impresses them. You cut a man's face and somebody asks you, "How many stitches?" "Twenty" you say, and they look at you—"Twenty? Only twenty? Christ, you hardly marked him." The next time you cut a face you make a bit more certain it will be news.

He turns aside and doubles up holding his head. Rock beat. BANDIT *and* SLUGGER *attend to him.*

BYRNE   Ma heid! Ma heid! Ma fucking heid! The bastard kept hitting it wae a hammer.
BANDIT   Never mind, Johnny. You made a mess o him.
BYRNE   Ah wus so angry ah didnae know whit ah wus daein. He's no deid, is he?
BANDIT   He's no deid, but you just aboot gouged his eye oot wae that screwdriver you were carryin.
SLUGGER   They're aw saying yir crazy. They're sayin yir a lunatic. They're aw scairt tae fuck o yae.

BYRNE   *Straightens up and thinks this over. Smiles.*

BYRNE   That's whit thair sayin is it? That ah'm a lunatic? That's awright then, isn't it? Ah ahm a lunatic. Ah'll dae anythin! You'se hud aw better watch it!

They are afraid of him for a moment. He stretches out his palm as at beginning of play.

16

Its just as well, eh? *Smiling*
BANDIT   *Smiling* Aye!
They slap hands. BANDIT *and* JOHNNY, SLUGGER *and* JOHNNY.
SLUGGER   *Slapping* We're aw in it thegither.
They are laughing. BANDIT *suddenly on the alert.*
BANDIT   Hey, look. Here's Big Danny coming. Somebody said he hud a
joab fur you, Johnny, doon at his shebeen.
SLUGGER   Yir going places, Johnny.
LIZZIE   *Looking out of her window* Johnny, you're a mug!
BYRNE *looks at her questioningly. Rock beat. Enter* BIG DANNY.

BANDIT   *With a flourish* Big Danny!
SLUGGER   Look at the suit! Get the material!

DANNY *is in his late forties. A flashy suit and tie, well-pleased with
himself. Smoking a cigar.*

DANNY   *To audience* They call me Big Danny and ah run a shebeen.
Dae yae's all know what a shebeen is? Well, its like Prohibition but its
no as big. In Glasgow, when these boys were still boys—before thae
goat too big fur their boots—the pubs closed up at nine o'clock. Nine
o'clock! Can you imagine it? So thir wur a loat o people wae drooths
oan thaim aboot the town and it wus a simple matter, if yae wantit tae
make some easy money, tae open up a wee place fur drinkin *efter* nine
o'clock. And that's exactly whit ah did. Up a close in the Gorbals. A
two room and kitchen. The place stacked wae bevvy. A shebeen! Ah
wus in business—fur ma sell.
—Hullo there, boys. Howzit goin?
BYRNE   No bad, Danny. How's things wae you?
DANNY   Business is good, boys, but it could be better.
BANDIT   Whit dyae mean, Danny?
DANNY   *Examining the tip of his cigar* Can ah ask youse boys a
question?
BYRNE   Fire away.
DANNY   How much ur youse makin in a week frae yir thievin?
BYRNE   How much? I don't know, Danny. We don't really keep count.
DANNY   Well, that's where youse ur makin a mistake because yae's
should keep count. Let's face it, boys, none o youse ur ever gonnae
work, ur yi?

17

B

BANDIT   Dead right we're no.

DANNY   Anyway, youse couldnae get a joab even if ye's wantit wan.

SLUGGER   Which we don't!

BYRNE   Ah hud a joab wance but it wus a waste o time, cooped up aw day wae somebody watching yir every move when yae could be oot oan the streets enjoyin yirsel . . .

DANNY   Aye. So whit else can ye dae but turn tae thievin. Yir hands are forced.

BANDIT   Nae option.

DANNY   A man's goat tae dae something tae keep himsel alive.

SLUGGER   An occupy his time . . .

DANNY   But wance ye've done that, yae've goat tae gie it some thoat. Wance a thief—always a thief. There's nae wae oot oh it. And yir maybe young now but youse'll soon be older.

BYRNE   Ah, come off it, Danny. Whit's aw this aboot?

SLUGGER   Aye, whit ur yae leading up tae, Danny?

DANNY   Oh, you'se ur clever boys alright. I can see that—except fur you, Byrne, everybudy knows you're a fuckin Hun. *They all find this funny*   so ah'll gie it tae ye's straight—how would youse boys like tae wurk fur me?

BANDIT   Wid we no just.

SLUGGER   Right an aw.

BYRNE   You two shut up and leave this to me. That wid depend, Danny.

DANNY   Whit wid it depend oan?

BYRNE   A loat o things.

DANNY   Like what?

BYRNE   Like what wid we be daein and whit wid you be payin us fur a start?

DANNY   Fur a start? Dae yae mean yae've goat mair conditions? Whit age ur you, Byrne?

BYRNE   Fourteen.

DANNY   Sweet Jesus, only fourteen and look ut him. Wahntin tae figure oot aw the angles before he's properly begun. Look, aw ahm lookin fur is somebody tae hang aboot in the streets at night ootside the shebeen tae bring the customers tae ma door. If youse boys urnae interested, ah can aye try somebody else.

BYRNE   Naebody else wurks in the streets in this part of town, and you know it.

BANDIT   Naebudy else wid dare.

18

BYRNE   Awright, so whit wid ye be payin us?

DANNY   Ah'm no sayin right now—but ah'll sae this, frae the look o you bunch an' the rags yir wearin, it'll be mair than yir making noo.

JOHNNY *is annoyed by this. It looks for a moment as if there might be trouble.*

An' there's no point in lookin ut me like that, Byrne. Ah'm gieing yae a chance. Ah'm gieing yae a chance tae better yirsel. Because ah can see ye've goat—talent. What's your answer?

BYRNE   We'll need tae discuss it.

DANNY   Awright, discuss it then. Is it gonnae take long?

BYRNE   Naw. Just gie us a few minutes...*Takes the others aside.* Listen... don't let him see you're too keen. we've goat tae get as much oot oh this as ... *Conversation gets quieter as* DANNY *steps forward to talk to audience.*

DANNY   Lamentable, isn't it? There ah was—wan big fool leading three young nitwits further intae the hole that he's in. You know what finally happened tae me? Ah didnae dae any big prison stretches, though ah wus in an oot the Bar-L same as the rest o them, but ah wus too weak tae be really crooked an ah took tae the boattle. If yae saw me nooadays it wid be oan a street coarner, wae stubble oan ma chin an ma clothes gone shabby—a hasbeen and a wino, gone beyond all hope. Ah didnae last long as bigshot ...

Returns to the boys.

...so. Hus the great cooncil come to its decision. Whit a huddle. Youse ur wurse than the City fuckin Chambers.

BYRNE   We'll dae it—if the money's right.

DANNY   The money'll be right. Don't you worry about that. Comoan an ah'll get yies some chips tae celebrate.

SLUGGER   Tony the Tally wullnae let us in his chippy.

DANNY   He wull if ah tell him tae.

BANDIT   Good oan yae, Danny. Ah'll huv a fish supper.

SLUGGER   Ah wahnt a black puddin. Wae a pickled onion.

BYRNE   Could you get us in the pub, Danny?

DANNY   Johnny Byrne, now you're wae me, Big Danny, a loat o doors that previously were closed will suddenly magically be open tae yae.

19

BYRNE   Aye? That sounds fine.

Enter DANNY. *He has a glass of whisky.*

DANNY   Johnny, you an the boys huv been daein a loat o good wurk fur me.

BYRNE   Yae can say that again, Danny. When you took me oan ah didnae know ah'd be brekkin jaws fur yae.

DANNY   Well, in this game, Johnny, sometimes yae've goat tae be firm.

BYRNE   Aye, or get somebody else tae be firm fur ye.

DANNY   Whit ur you complainin aboot? Yir gettin paid well enough, urn't yae?

BYRNE   Aye. Fur the time being anyway.

DANNY   Naw. No just fur the time being. There's a bit mair action comin your way, Johnny. Ah wahnt tae make you ma right-hand man.

BYRNE   That's wise o you, Danny.

DANNY   Is that aw you've goat tae say. God, you're a close wee bugger. Two years yae've been workin fur me and you've always been so silent. But when you speak ah can feel the evil weighing down on your every word. Can ah trust yae, Johnny?

BYRNE   Whit's that yae've goat in yir hand, Danny?

DANNY   Bevvy. Whit does it look like?

BYRNE   Can yae trust the bevvy, Danny?

DANNY   You must be jokin. Ah see too much of it.

BYRNE   Well, if ye cannae trust yirsel wae the bevvy, yae cannae trust yirsel wae me. Because it's no me or the bevvy you should be worryin aboot, it's yirsel . . .

DANNY   Aw, don't you worry about me. Ah'll see masell alright alright. Listen, did yae see that yin that owes me the hunner?

BYRNE   Aye, ah saw him.

DANNY   Whit did he huv tae say fur himsel?

BYRNE   He says his wife's pregnant and he's nae money. He says it'll take him another month or two.

DANNY   Whit did you say?

BYRNE   Ah said ah'd be back tae see him in a day or two.

DANNY   Did he get the message?

BYRNE   Whit dae you think?

20

DANNY Aye. That's because he knows ah don't mess around. If he disnae come up wae the lolly . . . You get down and fix that fucker fur me.

BYRNE Don't worry, Danny. Ah'll gie him a face like the map o Glasca.

Percussion. Rock rhythm. ARCHIE *is rolling a cigarette.* WOMAN *is offstage.*

WOMAN Archie, are you no comin tae bed?

ARCHIE Aye, ah'll be through in a minit, Jean. Just you go tae sleep.

WOMAN Naw. Yae sat up aw last night, noo yir at it agen. An yae canny stay away fae that windae. Whit's the matter wae yae? Ur ye in some kind of trouble? Is there somebody efter yae?

ARCHIE Naw, naw. Nuthin like that. Ah just cannae sleep these nights. Ah don't know whit it is. It must be wae the baby coming. Maybe I'm worrying.

WOMAN I'd 've thought you'd be used to it by this time.

ARCHIE *To audience.* When somebody's after you, you cannae sleep— unless you sleep wae one eye open. Every noise you hear from the street, could be the noise of him coming. Footsteps on the pavement. A car draws up. The wind shakes and rattles at the window. Sometimes you wish he could come, just tae get it over with, just to put an end to this waiting.

WOMAN Archie, are you coming tae bed or ur yae no?

Rock rhythms. DANNY *and* BYRNE.

DANNY Noo that you've been upgraded, whit wid yae like?

BYRNE *To audience* So there I was standing with the sole of my shoe flapping, the buttons off my shirt and big holes all over my vest, and he's asking me what wid ah like. A right good suit with right good material, a brand spanking new white shirt and a tie to match. A pair of handmade shoes that were sparkling with polish. I always wanted to look like he does . . .
To DANNY.
I want a suit!

DANNY A suit? Haw. Haw. I asked him what did he want and he said a suit! Awright, Johnny boy. First thing the morn's morn, down tae Isaac the Tailor . . .

They break and BYRNE *stands to attention. Enter* BANDIT *and* SLUGGER *carrying suit.*

WOMAN *She stands screaming at him.* Monster! Sadistic bloody monster! You cut ma husband's face to shreds!

Drums. BYRNE *is kitted out in suit. Eventually he stands resplendent.*

LIZZIE Yae never seen that fight last night, did yae?

MAGGIE Naw. Ah didnae. But big Mary Boyce wus tellin me about it at the steamie this mornin.

LIZZIE That Johnny Byrne half killed wan o those boys he wus fightin wae. Ah don't know how the poor soul managed tae pick hissel aff the ground the state he wis in.

MAGGIE That's the thurd fight this week. It's time that Johnny Byrne grew up so it is.

LIZZIE It's his maw ah feel sorry for. She works aw day fur those boys so she does. She must be heartbroken.

MAGGIE He's gonnae end up in Barlinnie the way he's goin. It's time he goat himsel a lassie an thoat aboot settlin doon.

LIZZIE Aye. Aw him an his pals dae is sit in that pub aw day long drinkin an swearin, an that gaffer o the pub's just as bad because he gies thaim drink fur nuthin.

MAGGIE He's just goan fae bad tae worse since he got in tow wae that Big Danny.

LIZZIE That wee niaff!

MAGGIE Ah think yir right, Lizzie. A lassie wid be the makins o that boy. Sometimes ah think its the only hope he's goat left.

Enter SLUGGER *and* BANDIT. BANDIT *looking around him.*

BANDIT Is Johnny no here yet? Its no like him tae be late.

SLUGGER He'll be wae the burd.

BANDIT Aye, probably. *Slightly derisive. Looks around him, taking in the audience.* Thair they go, Slugger, the honest workin people. Whit a bunch o mugs! They get up in the mornin and go oot tae wurk and get their miserable wages ut the end o the week tae help them pay fur their miserable wee hooses an' their miserable wee lives. Wance a year

22

they're released fur two weeks. The Glesca Fair! An' thae aw go daft! Eejits! Two weeks later its back tae the grindstone again fur another year.

SLUGGER   Either that or they cannae get a joab an' they go aboot in fuckin poverty.

BANDIT   Well thank Christ that's no fur us. When we want something— we take it. And it doesnae matter who it belangs tae.

SLUGGER   When we take it, it belangs tae us.

BANDIT   Aye and aw the toffs and intellectuals hate oor guts. Because we're the wans that kick in thir doors an climb in thir windaes and run oaf wae aw their nice new presies an their family hierlooms. An they know we don't give a fuck. Efter we've done a place an left it in a mess, ah'll bet they can still feel us in the air roon aboot thaim an they wonder who we are. What we're like. Because its obvious we don't give a fuck . . .

SLUGGER   Smash their shoap windaes in. Dynamite their safes. Chib thaim in the street ut night an' run aff wae their money! Naw. They don't like us. They don't like us at aw.

BANDIT   An thae cun stuff their fuckin probation officers up thur fuckin arses. *Pause.* Here's Johnny coming. Aw naw, he's goat hur wae him.

Enter JOHNNY *and* CAROLE. *Talking and laughing.* BANDIT *interrupts them.*

BANDIT   Hey, Johnny, fancy goin doon the Railway Club the night fur a bevvy?

CAROLE   I thought we were going out tonight.

BYRNE   Well, you can come alang wae us.

CAROLE   I thought we were going out by ourselves withoot thae two eejits.

Hits her.

BYRNE   Watchit, Carole. Ah've warned you before aboot cheekin me in front o the boys.

CAROLE   That's aw you worry aboot, isn't it? Yir reputation! Aw ahm good fur is cerryin yir chib an cop-watching fur yae.

BYRNE   Naw. That's no aw yir good fur.

CAROLE   Och, shut up you. You make me sick. Wan minit your aw affection, the next yir like a bluddy animal. You shouldnae tell me we're going oot if we're no.

23

SLUGGER   Oh, wid yae listen tae that. She'll be wahntin tae merry him next.

BYRNE   Right. Hurry up you if your comin.

CAROLE   Aw, piss off!

BYRNE   Cumoan, lads.

BANDIT   Aye, furget her, Johnny. Ah don't know whit yae see in hur.

BYRNE   Ah'm no asking you tae um ah?

BANDIT   Hey, fancy we'll go doon the Barrowland instead an pick up some burds.

SLUGGER   Nooky!

BYRNE   Aye, a fancy that. Haud oan. Hey, Carole, gie's ma chib.

CAROLE   Whit dae yae wahnt yir chib fur if yir just goin doon the Railway Club?

BYRNE   Never you mind. Just give us it an less o the questions. *She gives it to him* Right. Ah'll see you later. Right, lads. Doon the Barraland. If any o that Calton mob jump us, we'll be ready for them.

SLUGGER   An ah thoat we wur going doon fur some nooky . . .

BANDIT   *Triumphant* See yae later, Carole . . .

Exit BANDIT *and* SLUGGER. *But Byrne sits down behind* CAROLE, *with his back to her.* CAROLE *speaks to audience.*

CAROLE   Later. Later. That's aw ah ever hear. Aw ahm good fur is keeping his chib an cop-watching fur him. Everybody says ah need ma heid looked going aboot wae him. He's a dead cert road tae trouble, wan way or another. Ah'd like tae say that he was different when he wis wae me—quiet and gentle and affectionate like. But he's no. Ah suppose he must feel something for me—but if he does, he doesnae show it. Aw he's interestit in is his nookie then its doon tae the pub wae the boys.

BYRNE   Carole! Carole!

CAROLE   What's the matter?

BYRNE   Scratch ma back, Ah've goat a helluva itch.

CAROLE   Goad, yae never know the minit, dae yae? Whereaboots?

BYRNE   Just aboot there. That's it. Naw, a wee bit higher. Naw, lower. That's it. Oh, that's lovely . . . Rerr . . .

CAROLE   Here, leave me alane ya durty pig . . .

BYRNE   Stop it I like it . . .

24

CAROLE   Naw, really. Ah've goat soup oan an ah doant want it tae overheat. It loses aw the flavour.

BYRNE   Oh well, you go right ahead wae yir soup, hen. Don't let me stoap yae. Yae'll make somebody a good wife wan o these days.

CAROLE   Aye well maybe one day yae'll huv tae marry me!

BYRNE   Och don't talk stupid!

CAROLE   Ah'm no talking stupid. Did naebday ever tell you the facts o life?

BYRNE   Ah mean whut dae yae wahnt tae be married tae a character like me fur? Ma roads mapped oot fur me. Ah keep a chib over the door an a blade in ma bedroom. That's when ahm no oan the run or oot causin damage. Ah'm for the Bar-L. Its inevitable.

CAROLE   It doesnae need tae be inevitable, Johnny. Yae can change things, you know.

BYRNE   Aw, gie us a brekk, wullyae? What can ah change? Fuck all.

CAROLE   Well, maybe if yae were married an hud a family . . .

BYRNE   Ah'd huv tae feed thaem. Or you'd huv tae feed them's mair likely. Just like my ma hud four o us tae feed efter ma father died.

CAROLE   But Johnny, even if yae did dae a stretch, you could rely oan me. Ah widnae mess yae aboot.

BYRNE   That's whit yae say now, but it's a different story when it happens. Look ut Big Jean—her husband's daein four years. She managed tae keep hursel fur him fur a year and that wus that. She started shacking up wae somebody else. Wait till he gets oot.

CAROLE   Ur you comparin me tae that Big Jean?

BYRNE   Naw ah'm no comparin yae tae . . .

CAROLE   It sounds very much tae me as if yae ur . . .

BYRNE   Aw in the name o . . . You know something, Carole?

CAROLE   What?

BYRNE   Ah'd love a plate o soup.

Rock rhythms.

Enter SLUGGER, *speaks straight to audience.*

SLUGGER   Ah wus up in Duke Street buying masel a coupla flash shurts an there wus a gemme oan ut Parkheid. The Old Firm. Jesus Christ, whit a bunch o eejits—grown men throwin screwtaps at each uther frae wan side o the road tae the uther, an aw in the name o religion. Ah don't know whit that's supposed tae be aboot at aw. They wurk aw week then oan a Saturday thae go daft an split each other's heids open, then oan a Sunday thair oot tae twelve o'clock Mass un oan their knees. Sheer hypocrisy. *Enter* BANDIT.

BANDIT   Just so long as thair no taking money oot o oor pockets!

SLUGGER   Right an aw!

BYRNE   *Approaching them* Aye, but you'll let Danny take money oot o your pockets.

BANDIT   Whit dae yae mean? It's Danny thut pays us, in' it?

BYRNE   Is it? So far as ah can see, we pay oorsels—underpay oorsels. Danny might hand over the notes tae us ut the end o the week, but that's aw he does. You think aboot it, when we startet wae Danny, we wur just boys. That wus two years ago. An Danny wis just runnin the Shebeen. It wus easy wurk. Noo he's intae everythin—every racket that's going, he's goat his finger in the pie. An' its us he's using tae dae it. He's goat us breakin jaws fur him an' taking aw the risks, but we're no seein enough return fur it personally.

BANDIT   So whit yae sayin? We'll chin him fur mair money?

BYRNE   Aye. Something like that.

BANDIT   Supposing he says no.

BYRNE   Whether Big Danny says yes or no makes no difference anymore.

BANDIT   I'm beginning tae see whit yae mean.

Enter DANNY.

DANNY   Hello there, boys, howzit goin? Still enjoyin the good life?

BYRNE   Hello, Danny.

BANDIT   Hello.

SLUGGER   Hello.

DANNY   Hey, whit's this? Aw the hellos. Ur you boys claimin me?

BANDIT   Yir gettin awfa sensitive in yir old age, Danny.

DANNY   Less o the old . . .

BYRNE   Its just that me an' the boys huv been discussin money.

DANNY   Ah should ah guessed. Well, ah suppose youse ur entitled tae a rise wae the way things ur expandin . . .

BYRNE   We don't want a rise, Danny.

DANNY   Whit dae yae want then?

26

BYRNE   We're intae yae fur the loat. *Slashes him* We Rule, ya fool.
DANNY   O.K. . . .

Percussion. Pub lights up. DEADEYE *singing. Rock beat.* DEADEYE'*s voice is heard in the darkness.* LIGHTS *come up on the domestic area.* SLUGGER, BANDIT *and* JOHNNY *are seated, sharing a bottle of cheap wine with* DEADEYE. *Some of his swag is laying on the table.* DEADEYE *sings with his eyes closed, his arms outstretched. It is the Nat King Cole song "Too Young".*

DEADEYE   *Singing* And yet we're not too young to know . . .
   this love may last, though years may go . . .
   and then some day they may recall . . .
   we were not . . . too young . . . at all.

The boys laugh and cheer.

DEADEYE   *Encouraged* I know a millionaire, who's burdened down
   with care.
BYRNE   *Hastily interrupting him* Yir a good wee cunt, Deadeye, so yae
   urr.
DEADEYE   We're aw happy, int wi'? Ah mean we've aw earned a bit an'
   that's whit matters intit?
BYRNE   Mind any other swag yae get gie us a chance eh it first.
DEADEYE   Don't worry aboot that, Johnny. Ah know that if ah'm
   involved wae you an the mob, nae cunt's connae bump me fur ma
   money.
BANDIT   That's right, kiddo. An' you know none o us will bump yae.
DEADEYE   See that big bastard Sid doon ut the Bookies, he tried tae
   knock ma price doon ti fifteen bob by sayin' the material on the shirts
   wis shite. The big bastards worth a fortune as well.
BYRNE   Aye, he's a tight big bastard. Gie him nothin. He likes tae try
   and take liberties, an there's a loat o talk aboot him bein a grass.
BANDIT   Aye, that's right. He's supposed tae huv told the busies aboot
   wee Sniffer when he knocked him back fur some jewellery that he
   blagged.
BYRNE   Ah'll tell yae whit ah'll dae, Deadeye. Frae now on, don't bother
   dealing wae anybody else. Fae now on, any swag yi get gie me the

27

chance o it and yae can put the word roon aw the young yins that urr
blaggin swag an tell thaim that ah'll get thaim a good price fur it.

DEADEYE   Nae bother. Ah'll dae that. There's been too many cunts oot
tae bump me recently.

SLUGGER   *At a sign from* BYRNE *he is again bundling* DEADEYE *out.* Just
get the swag sent doon here an' we'll attend tae it.

DEADEYE   Right . . . Aye . . . *Confused*   Goodbye, Johnny.

BYRNE   Goodbye, Deadeye.

BANDIT   That's the right way, Johnny. Sew the whole district up. We
can earn a right few quid if we get these guys in hand. They blag some
ace gear.

SLUGGER *re-enters.*

SLUGGER   Auld cunt. Ah thoat he'd never stoap talkin. He wus wahntin
tae sing me another song oan the doorstep. Ah telt him tae wander.

BYRNE   Right, Slugger, sit doon. Ah wahnt tae talk tae yaes seriously
fur a change.

SLUGGER   Its aboot money. People only talk serious when they're
talking aboot money.

BYRNE   Cut it oot, Slugger. Right. Now look. Since we took over frae
Big Danny we've taken over his contacts. We're intae everythin. The
Docks. The Brasses. Protection. We've goat the loat. An' that's aw
right as far as it goes, but ah think we cun take it further.

BANDIT   Never satisfied!

BYRNE   Sure ahm no satisfied. Because ah've come to realise somethin
more and more strongly these days. We're no ut the thievin any more,
we're runnin a business.

SLUGGER   You don't say. We'll need tae turn the shebeen intae an office
then an pit oor names up on the door—J. Slugger, Company
Secretary. Knock Three Times—Heavily.

BANDIT   Yeah an' we could get ourselves a nice little secretary with nice
little tits and a waggly bum . . .

BYRNE   *Laughing* Awright! Awright! Ya pair o eejits! Anyway, aw ahm
leadin up tae the noo is tae say that ah wahnt us tae open a bank
account.

SLUGGER   A bank account! Not on your Nellie! You'll huv us paying
income tax next.

28

BYRNE   Naw. There's ways roon that. False credentials. You open an account in an assumed name.

SLUGGER   Frank Costello.

BANDIT   Luciano!

SLUGGER   Jesse James!

BANDIT   Billy the Kid!

BYRNE   *Laughing* Fucking Genghis Khan! Ya pair o eejits. Right, listen...

BANDIT   Naw. Wait a minute, Johnny. Ah think we get the point. That'll be aw fine and dandy tae huv a bank account and talk aboot the businees an aw that but...

BYRNE   *Annoyed and suspicious* But whit?

BANDIT   Well... do you no think you're going a wee bit far these days?

BYRNE   What are you talking about?

BANDIT   You know what ah'm talking aboot. Them two yae done over the other night wae a steakie, that's whit ahm fucking talking aboot an you know it. Wan o these days you're gonnae end up killin somebody.

BYRNE   What are you talking about?Whit's aw this aboot killin people? Huv you been drinkin?

BANDIT   You know fine well ah huvnae been drinking.

SLUGGER   An aw ah know is ah could be daein way wan right now. Cumoan tae fuck. You two wid ergue the hindlegs aff a donkey.

BYRNE   Awright. Cumoan then. You'll need tae watch that drooth o yours, Slugger. You'll be gettin a beer belly.

SLUGGER   Its better than a cut face, Johnny.

BYRNE   So's a loat o things. *Turns back to* BANDIT. Listen, Bandit, you must be mistaken. Ah never done over those two eejits the other night—ah don't use a steakie—did you furget that?

BANDIT   *Resigned* Anything you say, Johnny.

BYRNE   Right, cumoan then, pal. Doon tae the boozers.

Percussion. They cross stage to pub area.

BYRNE   Hiya, Carole.

CAROLE   Ah've been here a whole half hoor waiting fur you.

BYRNE   That's tough kid. Whit are yae drinkin?

SLUGGER   Ah'm gettin thaim, Johnny.

BYRNE   That cunt Kelly wus supposed tae be here the night. Ah wunder if he's gonnae show his face.

BANDIT   He's a month overdue us it is.

BYRNE   Ah think he'll come across wae the money awright but—ta, Slugger   SLUGGER *hands in drinks . . .* ah think we'll need tae gie him a nice receipt fur it when he does. Just a wee reminder that yae've got tae pay up promptly.

BANDIT   A receipt. Ha, ha. That's it. We'll give him a receipt!

CAROLE   Christ, an ah thoat we wur coumin here tae relax.

SLUGGER   We are relaxing, hen.

BANDIT   Oh, oh! Here he comes!

BYRNE   Oh. There he is. The very man ah wantit tae see. Ah wis hopin we might run intae ye.

KELLY   Aye, ah knew you'd be here. Ah heard yae wur lookin fur me. Ah've goat it here. Ah'm sorry its been so long in coming. But you know how it is.

BYRNE   Naw. Ah don't know how it is, Kelly. Tell me. You were supposed tae pay back a month ago.

KELLY   Ah loast it oan the betting, Johnny. Ah just didnae huv it tae gie ye, otherwise ah'd ah gied yae it wouldn't ah?

CAROLE   Fur fuck sake wid yae listen tae that?

BYRNE   You just keep yir mouth shut. *To* KELLY Right. Gie us it then.

KELLY   *Handing over envelope* There you are.

BYRNE   Count it, Bandit.

BANDIT   *A deft hand at running through the banknotes* Aye. Its aw here.

BYRNE   Right. Here's yir fucking receipt!

Sticks knife in KELLY's *face.*

The Windae-hingers

LIZZIE   Hullo, Maggie. That wis an awfae cerry-oan last night, did yae see it?

MAGGIE   Naw ah wus oot ut the Bingo. Whit wis it?

LIZZIE   There wis dozens o' squad cars an' polis raided houses an' shoaps aw o'er the district and there wis blue murder.

MAGGIE   In the name o Goad whit wus goin oan?

LIZZIE   Cun yae no guess? They liftit aw that Byrne crowd in a wunner—including that whore Carole.

MAGGIE   Whit ur thae daein thaim fur?

30

LIZZIE   Well, that big beat polis—no that ah can stand him either—but he was telling Jack in the Dairy that thir arrestin' thaim furr everythin under the sun.

MAGGIE   Ah thoat they wir payin' the polis aff and that wis how they never went near thaim at aw.

LIZZIE   Aye. And so did everybody else. But they've done the loat o thaim.

MAGGIE   Well, hell mend thaim. That's aw ah cin say. Hell mend thaim!

Windae-hingers withdraw. Enter BANDIT, SLUGGER *and* BYRNE. *They head for the pub.*

BANDIT   *Laughing* That really sickened thae bastards, didn't it?

SLUGGER   Aye. They'll no dig us up in a hurry again.

BYRNE   Ah don't know aboot that. We'll huv tae watch thaim.

BANDIT   The heid busy said he was chargin' me wae everythin under the book, but ah told him ahm sayin fuck all tae ah see ma lawyer.

SLUGGER   Aye. But ah wis worried. Ah thoat they wur gonnae dae a bit o' gardenin an start plantin some gear oan us.

BANDIT   Aye. They're better at that gemme than Percy Thrower.

BYRNE   Its just as well wee Rollo the lawyer goat there in time tae stoap them otherwise we'd be lyin in Bar by noo.

BANDIT   They really hate wee Rollo as he's the flyest mouthpiece in the business and is wide furr aw their gemms.

SLUGGER   Did yae see their faces when they hud tae let us go? It wus fuckin magic.

BYRNE   Aye but they meant business. And ah think they still mean business—especially wae me. They three I.D. Parades they gave us hid me worried. Ah thoaght they were gonnae stick some snide witnesses oanti' them tae dig us oot.

BANDIT   Aye. And imagine thaim puttin Big Kelly oan it. As if he wid dig us oot.

SLUGGER   They're fuckin idiots so they urr. Ah mean Kelly knows he deserved it. Ah cannae understand they busies.

They have entered the pub.

BANDIT   How's aboot a wee bit o service then?

BARMAN   Hullo thair, boys. Ah heard the cops dugyaes up.

31

BYRNE   Aye. You can say that again. Bastards! But lissen, seein' as things are a bit hoat furr us ah want yae tae keep these o'er the bar fur us.

Three of them start to unload weapons.

BARMAN   Aye, sure, son. Just gie thaim tae me. Ah'll look efter thaim fur ye.

SLUGGER   *Hauling out a meat clever* Noo ah don't wahnt you cuttin the heids affae pints, big yin!

BANDIT   Right noo ah've been lyin in a rotten cell aw weekend so ah want ah good bath, a burd and a right bevvy!

SLUGGER   Aye. An' we'll huv a right bevvy in here the night! *He mimics Elvis Presley.* Let's have a party... oh... oh... oh... let's have a party... ooh... ooh... ooh

BANDIT   *Taking him up on it and dancing in front of him* Dancing to the Jailhouse Rock... Bap!

He throws out his arms and sticks out his leg on the 'bap'. At exactly the same moment two policemen appear. SLUGGER *and* BANDIT *freeze on the spot.* JOHNNY *is drinking with his back to them.* SLUGGER *makes ineffectual attempts at speech—pointing at the police and opening and closing his mouth but saying nothing.* BANDIT *puts a hand on* JOHNNY's *shoulder.* JOHNNY *looks round and takes in the policemen. He stands up slowly. Rock rhythms begin. He faces the policemen, hands loose at his side. He walks towards them. They stand on either side of him. They walk out of pub.* BANDIT *and* SLUGGER *exit after them looking furtive and trying to hide. They exit in different directions as quickly as they can.*

The POLICE *leave* BYRNE *centre stage. He is handcuffed. He is standing to attention and expressionless. If possible, the next sequence should convey by lighting and flashes that* BYRNE *is having his photograph taken for police files. He is taken face on. Right profile. Left profile.* BANDIT *and* SLUGGER *look in on things furtively from either side of the stage. There is no joy in their chant.*

SLUGGER   Rats!
BANDIT   Rats aroon the backs!

32

SLUGGER   Rats aroon the backs an a wee dug!

BANDIT   It wus a rerr wee dug that.

SLUGGER   It kilt that many rats it goat a medal fur it.

BANDIT   It even goat a menshun in the paper.

Enter CAROLE.

CAROLE   Aye, boys. We're aw in it thegither. *Sarcastic.*

BANDIT   You shut up, ya cow. We'll keep things goin fur him while he's inside, an we'll stull be here waitin when he comes oot. Whit aboot you?

All three exit.

BYRNE   *To audience.* There is so much that none of you can understand about me and the world I come from and there doesn't seem to be any way of telling it that will finally get you to see the bitterness and indifference I inherited from whatever the system was the series of historical priorities that created the world into which I was born.

I didn't think. I didn't think much about it. I didn't say—there's a system—and analyse it—I was never taught to do that. But I felt. I felt strongly.

There were the haves and the have-nots. I was one of the have-nots. There were the have-nots that worked and the have-nots that thieved, then there were the rest of you—living away out there somewhere in your posh districts in aw your ease and refinement—what a situation!

It made me laugh to see you teaching your religions and holding your democratic elections—and it made me sick with disgust. That was why I enjoyed the sight of blood because, without knowing it, it was your blood I was after.

My first prison sentence was like going to university. I made a lot of new friends and useful contacts and we talked and planned together for the future. It was a top-level conference fur the world I moved in, and fur me it lasted all of two years. Maybe you'd hoped it would teach me a lesson and ah wid 'mend ma ways' so to speak. Well, it did teach me a lesson o sorts. When ah goat oot o that prison ah was ready fur somethin new—something ah had learned tae call "crime". Organised crime.

33

C

POLICE *re-enter and march* BYRNE *off. Action moves to next scene—* BANDIT *and* SLUGGER *in the pub. Drinking pints.*

SLUGGER   It'll no be long tae Johnny gets oot o' Bar-L noo.

BANDIT   Aye. Ah'll be glad tae see him hame again. Mind'ye he wis lucky only gettin two years fur bladin two guys.

SLUGGER   Ur you kiddin? It wis a fuckin liberty. He hud nae form.

BANDIT   Whit dyae mean? He's done his remand home, approved school and his Borstal.

SLUGGER   Aye but he's never been in Bar before.

BANDIT   Bit it wus a wee sentence fur the High Court.

SLUGGER   The last time ah saw him he wus daein his nut aboot Carole. Somebody hud telt him she wis oot at the dancin and he's no pleased aboot it.

BANDIT   Ah wunder who could ah telt him that.

SLUGGER   Ah wunder. Its no as if he's goat a loat o visitors.

BANDIT   Ach, Carole. She's a cow. She's never away fae the Barrowland an' aw that mob in the Calton urr ridin' hurr.

SLUGGER   You better no let him hear that when he gets hame.

BANDIT   Ah'm gonnae tell him. Ah'm gonnae tell him she's a midden. She deserves aw thats comin tae her.

SLUGGER   It's no Carole ah'm thinking aboot, it's Johnny. It'll break his heart.

BANDIT   That yin doesnae huv a heart. He's an animal.

CAROLE *in domestic area, putting on her eye shadow. Enter* JOHNNY. *He stands staring at her. Silent.* CAROLE *is using a small mirror. She sees him in it.*

CAROLE   Johnny! *Flings down eyeshadow brush.* Naebody telt me yae were gettin oot!

BYRNE   Did thae no?

CAROLE   Oh, Johnny. It's great tae see you again.

She runs to him and puts her arms round him. JOHNNY *pulls them away again.*

CAROLE   Whit's wrang, Johnny. Lissen, don't believe whit that Bandit says. He's just jealous. Ah've been faithful tae yae. Ah huvnae been up tae enythin . . .

34

BYRNE   *Looks her up and down, taking in her clothes and her make up.*
Aye. It looks like it.

*He moves towards her raising his clenched fist. He is wearing a knuckle
duster.*

CAROLE   Naw, Johnny. No ma face!

Enter SLUGGER *and* BANDIT *dressed in trilbies. Long, dark double-
breasted coats.*

BANDIT   *To audience.* Mr Byrne is going places!
SLUGGER   He's in wae the Firm, the Big Boys noo. *Arms out imitating
an aeroplane.* They fly him doon tae London. Thae meet him wae a
limousine. The biggest villains in Britain.
BANDIT   And everything is very cordial. Everything is very English.
SLUGGER   Everything is layed oan—booze, gamblin, women—the loat!
Nooadays oor Johnny wahnts fur nuthin!
BANDIT   An whit does he dae fur it aw in return? Just a wee bit o
business.
SLUGGER   Technical business!

Enter BYRNE *behind them with gun. He aims it around the audience, arm
outstretched. Then smiles, twirls it in his hand and puts it in his pocket.
Goes to* BANDIT *and* SLUGGER.

SLUGGER   You know your trouble. Yae never hud enough toys tae play
wae when yae wur a wean.
BYRNE   Where's the fancy-dress party then?
BANDIT   Aye, dyae like the toags. We goat them aff wee Isaac the Tailor
fur a laugh tae see yae aff at the airport.
BYRNE   Ah think the man ahm gonnae meet wid like thaim. Gie's a
shoat. *Snatches hat from* SLUGGER's *head.*

BYRNE *is moving his head from side to side jokily with the hat on. But the
other two have caught his last remark.*

35

BANDIT Who ur yae gonnae meet?

BYRNE *Straightening out, hat on his head, gun in his hand to punctuate the words.* George Raft!

SLUGGER Naw, cumoan, Johnny. Tell us. Who ur you gonnae meet?

BYRNE *Taking hat off and replacing gun in pocket.* George Raft. Ah'm tellin yae. The Mafia.

BANDIT Ur you serious?

BYRNE Did yae ever know me tae tell a lie? The Mafia wahnt tae move in oan the gamblin club scene in this country an' Glasgow's wan o the target areas. They wahnt tae talk tae me because they wahnt tae keep the local boys happy wherever they go.

BANDIT *Suspicious* That's awfae big o them, is it no?

BYRNE Its because they know if they don't cut us in they'll never get a minute's peace!

SLUGGER Too fuckin true they widnae. Scotland fur the Scoats. Heeuch!

Bandit has detached himself from the conversation. He is looking away from the other two.

BANDIT Aye, well that'll be aw fine an hunky-dory then wulln't it—if it aw comes aff. But the business in Glesca will huv tae go oan notwithstanding. Jist as it hud tae when you were in prison. An tonight—oan the eve o your departure fur the Big Smoke—there's wan ur two small local matters outstanding thut only Mr Byrne cun attend tae in his own inimitable style.

SLUGGER Hear aw the big wurds?

BYRNE What ur you tawkin about?

BANDIT Ah'm tawkin about those two eejits up in the Cowcaddens. They've been goin aroon extortin ut the pitch an toss pools fur months—oor pitch an toss pools—an you're lettin thaim get away wae it because they've been making a name fur themself o'er where they cum fae as a coupla real hard tickets!

BANDIT looks at BYRNE challengingly.

BYRNE Ur you wahntin yir face smashed in, Bandit?

BANDIT Aye. Yae cun smash ma face in if yae wahnt tae, Johnny, ah'm no disputin that—but it'll no get yae anywhere. Because you're

36

slippin. You've goat that fond o yir shooter an yir fancy new pals in London thut people ur sayin yir losin yir touch. Like you say, we're aw init thegither and ah'm just thinkin aboot yir reputation because there's a helluva loat depends oan it.

BYRNE   *Serious. Silent. Considers it all for a moment. Speaks at first as if chastened.* Aye, well maybe there's something in what you say— *Pause. Suddenly has* BANDIT *by the collar and is snarling in his face.* But ah don't like yir way o fuckin sayin it!

Holds BANDIT *by the throat for a moment then lets his hand fall and smiles, suddenly relaxed again.*

BYRNE   *Smiling.* Right. Where ur these eejits. Take me to thaim.

Twitchy rock thing from the drums. Billy Cobham. They produce different weapons and begin to lark about, stabbing and flailing at one another. SLUGGER *grabs* BANDIT'*s head under his arm and pretends to punch it with big elaborate gestures.*

SLUGGER   *Twisting* BANDIT'*s head about and smiling to audience.* He wouldn't give me his lollipop so I broke his left arm! He still wouldn't give me his lollipop so I broke his right arm! And when he continued with his obstinate refusal I broke his legs, his neck, his nose, his heid, smashed in his teeth, an made his mooth tae bleed an ah goat the fuckin lollipop so there!

BYRNE *is standing away from this smiling as if inspired. He has a knife in his hand. He says his words as if inspired by the knife and the general presence of violence like electricity in the air, (but not too inspired).*

BYRNE   So there! So there!

BANDIT *suddenly frees himself jumps up with a karate chop and howling all the way like in a Kung Fu film. From this* BANDIT *and* SLUGGER *go into a Karate routine.* BYRNE *starts singing vehemently.*

BYRNE   When somebody loves you Its no good unless he loves you *Lunging with knife* All . . . the . . . Way . . .

Suddenly they have all frozen. The drums have stopped. BYRNE *has dropped his knife. They are looking over their shoulders as if being pursued and in fact we are back at the beginning of the play when we first met the Boys. They have stopped for a moment, breathless, looking back.*

BANDIT   Oh my God! Oh ... my ... God!
BYRNE   *annoyed.* Whit's the matter wae yae?
BANDIT   Whit dae yae think?
SLUGGER   Aye. Naebody sed enythin aboot fuckin murder!

Domestic interior. JOHNNY *and the Big Brass.*

DIDI *sits with her legs up on the table, flexing one to help her fix the ladder in it with a brush of nail-polish.*

DIDI   Whit ah night ah've hid. Doon the Squerr. Wan efter another. Each wan mair pissed than the wan before. An it freezin. Ah hud oan this wee short skirt an ma arse wus like ice. Wan o ma regulars says tae me "Christ, Didi, yir tits ur blue!" *Thinks* He's no a bad soul that yin. He aye hus a wee drink fur yae. Ah'll say that fur him. Even if it does take him hoors sometimes just tae get it up. Aw its a hard life. Ah'm another social service. Creative leisure's ma department fur aw the poor bastards thur urnae gettin it elsewhere in the natural wey o things—an ah earn every penny that ah make, you take it from me. A hard life and a dangerous wan. Ma mate Big Elsie she ust tae go aboot in Glesca the same as me wae hur big boots an hur whip under hur belt fur aw the kinky wans. But she wus a junkie—that's the kind o thing this joab makes yae dae—if yir no a junkie yir an alcoholic or yir aff yir heid ur somethin—an she ust tae dae a bit o special business doon in London frae time tae time just tae relieve the monotony, aye, well she endit up in a bedsit in Notting Hill strangled wae hur ain nylons ...

JOHNNY *shouts in to her.*

BYRNE   Didi! Didi!

38

DIDI   Who's that ut this time?

BYRNE   Its me. Johnny Byrne. Let me in quick.

DIDI   *Opening up.* Oh Goad, yae nivir know the minit, dae yae? BYRNE
comes in. Ur yae awright?

BYRNE   Aye ahm fine. Close the door.

DIDI   What's happened?

BYRNE *relaxes. Recovers composure. Smiles.*

BYRNE   Nothins happened. Ah've just come roon tae see yae. Huvn't ah
aye telt yae yir ma favrit Big Brass?

DIDI   Oh yae've telt me awright often enough but ah don't ever see yae
unless yir in trouble. Sit doon. Wid yae like a drap o wine?

BYRNE   Aye. That wid be rerr, Didi.

DIDI   *Extracting a bottle of Eldorado from her handbag and pouring it
into cups.* Where's Carole the night then?

BYRNE   Hingin tae mae lip!

DIDI   Aye ah widnae be surprised if she'd followed you here.

BYRNE   Ah very much doubt it.

DIDI   Johnny, whit's wrang wae yir hand? Yir bleedin. Christ, whit's
been happenin, yir soaked in blood! Oh my fuck un ah huvnae a
bandage nor an elastoplast in the whole place. Here, wait an ahll get a
towel!

BYRNE   Its awright, Didi.

DIDI   *She has towel.* Its no awright at aw!

BYRNE   Its no ma blood ... *She withdraws from him. He smiles.* Ah
huvnae goat a mark on me.

Straight into next scene, pub interior. BYRNE *rapping to* SLUGGER *and*
BANDIT

BYRNE   OK. Right. So while ah'm away ah'm relyin oan you two tae
keep things goin. There'll be a loat o money-lendin an protection tae
collect ut the end o the month, and you've goat tae make sure its paid
up promptly. Ah wahnt you tae cover the docks, Slugger, and Bandit,
you dae aw the far away places wae strange-soundin names. Oh aye an
wan o yae tell Big Wilson o'er in Partick tae screw the nut. He's still
feudin wae the Anderson mob. Tell him there's supposed tae be an

Amnesty. The Law ur bamboozled becos we're no aw fightin wan another eny mair.

BANDIT   We can hardly tell him that now!

BYRNE   You know sometimes you really get on my nerves, Bandit.

BANDIT   Forget it, then. Sorry ah spoke. You an yir fuckin blood lust. It makes yae say wan thing an do another. Whit aboot Grangemouth?

BYRNE   Whit aboot Grangemouth?

BANDIT   They sed thair wid be a consignment of whisky comin in if we wur interestit we could huv it cheap.

BYRNE   Cheap enough tae make it worth oor while? How many boatles?

BANDIT   Mair than enough.

BYRNE   You'd better take a van.

SLUGGER   Aye. Yae cun hire wan frae Hertz.

BANDIT   Fuck Hertz. Ah'll nick wan doon the street.

Enter CAROLE *slowly. Her face is marked.*

SLUGGER   Look who it is!

BYRNE *and* BANDIT *turn and see her.*

CAROLE   Johnny, can ah speak tae yae oan yir ain?

BYRNE   Ah thoat ah telt yae tae fuck off. Ah'm no wahntin tae waste ma time talkin tae you, ya whore.

CAROLE   But it's important, Johnny. It's urgent.

BYRNE   Right then. If its aw that urgent tell me it right here and now. Then get tae fuck.

CAROLE   The Law ur lookin fur yae. Tae pick yae up.

BANDIT   Och, don't give us yir worries, Carole. We've goat the Law paid aff fur miles aroon.

SLUGGER   It'll be Constable McWhirter lookin fur mair bribes.

CAROLE   It wusnae the usual polis, Johnny. They wur roon ut the hoose askin questions.

BANDIT   *Mimics her.* It wusnae the usual polis, Johnny.

BYRNE   *To* BANDIT. You shut yir mouth. *To* CAROLE Whit did thae wahnt?

CAROLE   Thae wahntit tae know if ah'd been ut that party in Cowcaddens where the man was murdered.

BYRNE   Oh aye. And how did ma name get involved?

40

CAROLE   They thoat ah wus thair wae you.

BYRNE   An what did you say?

CAROLE   Ah sed ah hudnae seen yae and ah didnae no nothin about it.

BYRNE   Then whit did yae dae?

CAROLE   Ah came straight doon here tae warn you.

BANDIT   *Derisive.* Fur fuck's sake. Did yae leave a trail o breadcrumbs behind yae as yae came?

CAROLE   Johnny, they said they wur gonnae get you on this wan. They're determined.

BANDIT   Ah think you'd better catch that plane, Johnny.

BYRNE   *On his feet.* Right. Get in touch wae Rollo the Lawyer an' tell him he might be needit.

SLUGGER   *Exits.* Ah'll go an get the car.

CAROLE   Johnny, you wur up in Cowcaddens that night, wurn't yae?

BYRNE   Naw. Ah wusnae near the place, wus ah, Bandit?

BANDIT   Naw!

BYRNE   They're just tryin tae hustle me because thae don't like the money-lendin.

CAROLE   Johnny, ah'm worrit aboot yae.

BANDIT   Yir a bit late in the day fur that, ur yae no?

BYRNE   You wait outside, Bandit.

BANDIT   Awright, but hurry up. Remember they might be roon here enytime.

BANDIT *exits.*

BYRNE *takes* CAROLE's *face in his hand.*

BYRNE   That's an awfu bad mark you've goat thair. Did somebody hit yae?

He kisses her.

BANDIT   Ur you two comin or ur yae's gonnae staun thair snoggin aw night?

BYRNE *alone on stage.*

BYRNE   Alright. You can look down your nose at my moneylending. But the fact was I was providing a social service. When the police

41

finally got me they took away my address book with over three thousand addresses in it. They interviewed every person on that list but not one of them would give evidence against me. Not one of them. Because I'd been prepared to do business with them when you hadn't. While you were sitting back pretending not to notice, I had been there to care for their needs. Alright, my methods with defaulters were quick and to the point, but they weren't any different from your precious world—just a bit less hypocritical and undisguised.

Let's face it. The whole human world is a money-lending racket and if it takes a man's whole lifetime to kill him with his debts, that doesn't make it any the less an act of murder!

Explosion. SLUGGER *and* BANDIT *run across stage behind* BYRNE.

WOMAN'S VOICE   Leave us in peace! Hus there no been enough trouble already?

SLUGGER   You tell that man o yours tae keep his fuckin mouth shut or we'll be back.

Exit SLUGGER *and* BANDIT. *Enter Clerk of Court. Police come on and handcuff* BYRNE. *He stands, on trial.*

CLERK   *To audience.* My occupation is Clerk of Court. Three times I saw that man Byrne on trial for murder and twice I saw him get away with it. Witnesses disappeared. Testimony was withdrawn. Anyone who might speak against him was terrorised into silence and justice was thwarted.

On the third occasion, however, he was found Guilty: him and his cronies and his lawyer with him. It was third-time-lucky. When the Judge pronounced the sentence of life imprisonment for murder, I turned to the press benches, and the police, and even for a moment to the public gallery—and raised my thumb in triumph.

He has his thumb up and he presses it out victoriously on three sides of him.

The windows open and LIZZIE *and* MAGGIE *appear.* SLUGGER *and* BANDIT *come on the stage, putting on prison officer's uniform.*

42

LIZZIE So Byrne's goat life imprisonment right enough.

MAGGIE Aye and its good riddance tae bad rubbish. That's aw ah can say.

LIZZIE Aye. There must huv been en evil streak in him somewhere. Its the likes o him get the Gorbals a bad name.

MAGGIE Aye. *Pause.* Whit dyae think o that? The price o meat goin up agane?

LIZZIE Oh aye. Is it no awful? Ma man says ah should make omelettes. Ah says tae him, cun yae show me how? An he did. He made the tea last night. Omelette an chips. He said he learnt it when he wus daein his national service.

MAGGIE Aye. It's a pity that yin, Byrne, nivir hud any national service tae dae. That wid huv knocked the nonsense oot his heid.

SLUGGER *and* BANDIT *are now dressed in full prison officer uniform. They stand officially on either side of* BYRNE. *They have become the prison wardens.*

BYRNE *To audience* I did not do the crime I was convicted for.

Drums. SLUGGER *and* BANDIT *march off the stage with* BYRNE. *The* CLERK OF COURT *follows behind—a little man, by the way—smiling to the audience. The Windae-hingers withdraw.*

SONG The Sweetest of Songs is the Song of the Clyde.

End of ACT ONE

BYRNE *on bunk. Prison cell.* MOCHAN *in next cell listening.* BYRNE *direct to audience.*

BYRNE When a man goes into prison, he's suddenly cut off. His old friends disappear, and his wife, his family—how can he possibly keep in touch wae them when he's locked away.

He hears that his son's getting into trouble, following in his father's footsteps, but he can do nothing about it. The walls prevent him. The thick walls of justice. Your justice.

Enter JOHNSTONE, *Prison Officer. Furtive*

JOHNSTONE Byrne! Byrne! You're a faither. Your burds just hud a baby.

BYRNE When?

JOHNSTONE Last night. Its a girl.

BYRNE A girl? Ur they awright?

JOHNSTONE Aye, they're fine. There's somebody coming, I'll need to go. *Exits*

BYRNE Naw. Don't go. Come back. Listen! Listen!

To audience So yir daein time. That's a good phrase for it. Daein time. Because that's whit yir daein awright. Time! Time with no distractions. Plenty of time tae consider the matter. Time tae burn. Time tae waste. Time tae kill.

One year. Two year. Three year. Four.

And if yir lucky you've goat a window you can see through, and if you're even luckier through that window you can see a tree, and you think about the day when you'll see the other side of that tree.

Beans. Sweat. Urine. Insomnia.

Tries to catch a fly

44

Poor me. Poor fly. Sharing a cell.

Five year. Six year. Seven year. More.

Thick. Thick. Walls of justice.

Thick. Thick. Heads of justice.

Thick. Thick. Assholes of justice.

Thick. Thick. Whores of justice.

—who do you think you are locking me up in here and telling me it's for life? Telling me I deserve it? My life. Fullstop. Thank you very much. I'm so grateful to you for giving me what I deserve. It must be nice to be in the right because it's shitty to be in the wrong.

JOHNSTONE   Your lawyer's here for you, Byrne.

BYRNE *turns as Lewis, lawyer, enters.*

LEWIS   Sorry I couldnae get here sooner, Johnny. How are you?

BYRNE   In a wee bit o a hurry tae get oot o here.

LEWIS   They've put you in solitary.

BYRNE   Aye well there's a fly up in the corner up there. He an me huv been huving a wee bit o a blether. How's Carole?

LEWIS   She's fine, Johnny. She's at home with her mother.

BYRNE   That old bag. Tell hur no tae be giein the wean any o her cheap biddy.

LEWIS   Does she drink?

BYRNE   The old woman? Christ, she'd drink the Clyde dry if it wis full o whisky.

LEWIS   You don't need to worry about the baby. Carole will look after her alright. You can trust her.

BYRNE   Trust her nothing. Lewis, ah wahnt out o here and fast. Ah lay doon oan ma bunk last night and a thoat, fifteen years. Fifteen fuckin years. That old swine ae a judge an' the police lieing their mooths aff. How long wull it take fur the Appeal tae come through?

LEWIS   Johnny, I wouldnae pin any hopes on an appeal. They were out tae get you. One way or another. The walls of that court would have had to fall down before you'd have walked out of there a free man.

JOHNNY *is silent.*

I don't suppose you'll have seen your press.

45

BYRNE *Reading* "I was a victim of The Gentle Terror!" Whit's aw this about?

LEWIS Did you no know? That's the name you go under in the Glasgow underworld. Read further down.

BYRNE "Father of four William Brown told of the night he was threatened by . . . John Byrne, better known as The Gentle Terror, who said that if he didn't pay his debt, he would cut off his ears!" Jesus Christ! These people have got wonderful imaginations!

LEWIS You're good copy, Johnny. There's no a good word to say about yae.

BYRNE And will that affect the appeal?

LEWIS Well, it shoudnae but it gives you an indication. They're gloating, Johnny. And now they've got you, they're no gonnae let you go without a struggle. The best you can hope for is a bit of remission and parole from time to time—if you keep your nose clean. And your hands to yourself. I know it won't be easy but I would be misleading you if I told you otherwise.

BYRNE *silent, thinking*

BYRNE Why did they put me in solitary, Lewis?

LEWIS Because of your reputation, Johnny. You're a dangerous man.

Pause. BYRNE *thinks again before he speaks.*

BYRNE Aye. Well, ah'm no gonnae stop being dangerous, just because ah'm in here. If thae think ahm gonnae crawl fur a bit o parole, they've goat another think comin.

LEWIS A few years ago they would have hanged you.

BYRNE They're gonnae wish they hud.

Enter MOCHAN, *sweeping the stage*

MOCHAN Hello there. Ma name's Michael Mochan. Ah've goat a story too. But youse'll no be wantin tae be bothert wae that. Ah mean, ah'm just an old lag, who wahnts tae know whit ah think? Ah dae keep ma nose clean *wipes it* so ah get wee joabs tae dae an ah get aboot mair

46

than the rest o thaim. An that way ah get tae hear a loat an' see a loat, an usually ah keep my mooth shut aboot it, but wae the things that happened tae that man, Byrne, well, the time came when ah knew ah couldnae just sit back and watch any loanger, ah wis gonnae huv tae say whit ah hud seen, whatever it cost me . . . No that it made much difference.

Pause. Thinks Ach, but that aw comes later when ah goat tae know him. So ah'll talk tae yaes later oan—if that's awright. Ah jist thoat ah'd say hello an introduce masel.

Exits

BYRNE *and* CAROLE *and* JOHNSTONE

BYRNE   Where's the wean?
CAROLE   Ah left hur wae ma muther.
BYRNE   Yae whit? Ur ye aff yir heid?
CAROLE   Ah knew yae'd wahnt tae see hur but ah wus feart she catch the cauld.

BYRNE *is exasperated. He looks at* JOHNSTONE *who is standing by.*

BYRNE   Can you no wait ootside fur a while?
JOHNSTONE   Sorry Johnny. Ah've goat ma orders.   •
BYRNE   Aye, awright. Yir no a bad cunt, Johnstone. Ah wish there were mair like you in this shithoose. *To* CAROLE It wus him telt me aboot the wean. Otherwise ah'd never huv known. That's the way they treat you in this fuckin place. Huv yae seen Danny?
CAROLE   He's lying low.
BYRNE   Ah'll bet he is, the old bastard. The rest o us inside an' he goes Scotfree. Typical. Ah'll bet he's drinking himsel paralytic. Old swine.
CAROLE   Thae wur aw tawkin aboot you in the hoaspital.
BYRNE   Wur they?
CAROLE   Aye. Aw the women. Lying thair feeding thair weans an you wur the main topic o conversation. You should ah heard the things thae wur sayin.
BYRNE   Ah've seen the papers.
CAROLE   It wus worse than the papers. Wan wife sed yae impaled somebody on the spike o a railin, another wan said yae tortured a man

47

by nailing his feet tae the floor. An thir wus this big fat bitch thair, it was hur eigth, and she sed you wur a hired gun doon in London.

BYRNE An whit did you say?

CAROLE Ah never said anythin. Ah kept ma mooth shut.

BYRNE Ur yae ashamed o me then?

CAROLE Well, whit dae yae expect me tae dae, haud the wean up an tell them you loat just watch whit yir sayin Byrne's this wean's father.

BYRNE Well you might've stoaped them tellin lies aboot me at least.

CAROLE How dae ah know if its lies. Ah don't know how many people you've kilt, dae ah?

BYRNE Well ah'll tell yae. Ah've never kilt anybody in ma fuckin life— and don't you furget it. CAROLE *Looking away. Then to* JOHNSTONE— Can ah gie him a cigarette? JOHNSTONE *nods assent. She produces cigarettes from her bra.*

BYRNE Whit ur yae daein?

CAROLE Thae take everythin aff yae doon thair. *Lights cigarette for him. One for herself*
That yin Halliday's cerryin oan like a big shoat noo that you're inside.

BYRNE Whit's he daein?

CAROLE He wus in the pub last night an he smashed the gantry.

BYRNE Eeejit!

CAROLE Tommy the barman says thair aw fighting like cats an doags because you're no thair tae keep the peace.

BYRNE Aye well you tell Tommy ah'll see tae thaim soon enough.

CAROLE How come?

BYRNE Because ah'm getting out o here, that's how come.

CAROLE Naebday telt me aboot it. When ur yae getting out?

BYRNE Ah'll no bother, if that's how you feel aboot it. Ah'll just stay here.

CAROLE Och don't talk stupit!

BYRNE Whit's the matter wae you? Huv yae goat yirsel a new man awready?

CAROLE Look ah huvnae goat time tae look fur fellas, ah'm too busy lookin efter your fuckin wean.

BYRNE *raises his arm.* JOHNSTONE *moves to restrain him.*

BYRNE Aw, don't worry, Johnstone, old boy. She's no worth it. Ur yae married yirself?

48

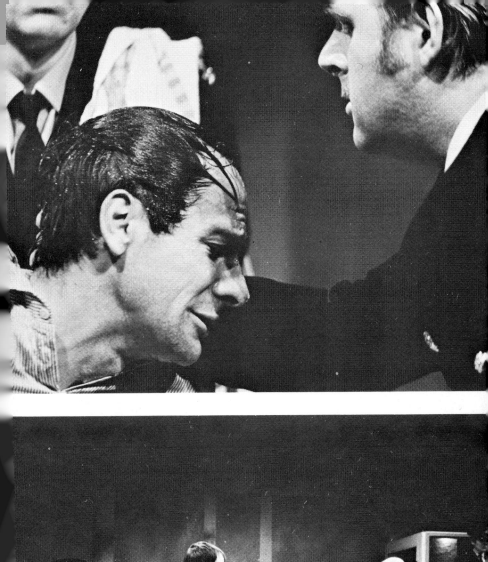

JOHNSTONE Aye.

BYRNE Any family?

JOHNSTONE A boy and a girl.

BYRNE Good fur you!

CAROLE Wull you stoap talking tae that swine an tell me whit this is aw aboot?

BYRNE Whit? Oh, ur you still here? Awright, ah'll tell yae. Now listen carefully fur wance in yir life. This is important. Its aboot ma Appeal.

CAROLE Oh, is that aw.

BYRNE Whit dae yae mean "is that aw"?

CAROLE Well, Lewis hus telt me aw aboot it.

BYRNE Lewis doesnae huv enything tae dae wae it anymore.

CAROLE Huv yae changed yir lawyer?

BYRNE Aye.

CAROLE Who huv yae goat? Franchetti?

BYRNE That balloon. You must be jokin.

CAROLE Who then?

BYRNE Maself.

CAROLE You? Since when did you become a lawyer?

BYRNE *Sits back and regards her with disgust.* Look ut yae, ya stupit wee whore. Of course ah'm no a lawyer, fur fuck sake. Ah'm no pretendin tae be a lawyer, but can you no understand anything? Do you no understand anything at all? No even aboot me?

This is ma life ah'm fighting fur. You've hud a wean tae me an ah wahnt tae see it. No in here. Ah'm glad you didnae bring it in here. Because ah don't wahnt it tae see its faither in a place like this.

CAROLE It happens to be a she.

BYRNE Ah thoat a telt you tae listen.

CAROLE Awright, ah'm listening.

BYRNE OK. This is ma life ah'm fightin fur and nobody can fight fur ma life except me maself. But ah'm gonnae need new witnesses and ah wahnt you tae talk tae a few people fur me. Do you understand that?

CAROLE Which people?

BYRNE *Hesitates. Speaks to* JOHNSTONE. Could you stoap up yir ears fur a minit, Johnstone?

JOHNSTONE Ah'm afraid the time's up, Johnny.

BYRNE Aye but we've goat drinkin up time. *Returns to* CAROLE Go doon tae the pub and talk tae the Big Yin.

CAROLE Wullie?

49

D

BYRNE   Aye! An' tell him tae talk tae that mob in Shamrock Street an tell thaim ah'll be wahntin tae see thaim up here.

CAROLE   Who do you mean in Shamrock Street?

BYRNE   Never mind that. Just tell him. He'll know whit ahm talking aboot.

JOHNSTONE   Awright, that's the time.

CAROLE   *Annoyed at* JOHNSTONE. Och, awright. Ah'm just goin.

BYRNE   Come here. *She goes to him.* Dae's a favour Johnstone an close yir eyes a wee minit.

They kiss

Noo don't you furget that. And next time bring the wean in so that ah can see it.

Enter MOCHAN.

MOCHAN   The course of young love never runs smooth. Aye, well he's making a big mistake handling that Appeal himsel. They'll no like that. There was only one man ah ever knew that managed to really speak the truth in a Court of Law and that wus an old wino ah knew. A right old down-and-outer, reeling aboot in the streets wae a three-week stubble oan his chin an stoapin people fur the price of a cup o tea. An niver even goat tae know his name. But ah saw his grand finale in the Sheriff Court in Glasgow wan day, when he goat tae his feet swayed fae side tae side straightened himsel up took a deep breath an made a speech oan his own behalf. This wus him:

Today ah wish tae apologise. Ah wish tae apologise tae ma wife fur the terrible life ah gied hur tae ma children—who no longer want to speak to me—fur aw they hud tae go without because of their father—tae aw the people—doctors and police social workers and ministers of religion—who tried tae give me help only tae huv the help thrown back in their face and most of all—most of all, he said, and he swayed a wee bit—most of all ah want tae apologise tae this Court in its Mercy fur the many times ah spurned its Clemency. Ah apologise!

The whole Court was stunned intae silence. And the Sheriff leaned forward and said, "Is there anything you would like to add?" And the old fella looked up and he smiled and he opened out his arms and he closed his eyes tilted back his head, and this is whit he said: *Sings*

50

I left my heart
In San Francisco...

BYRNE Your Worship, Ladies and Gentlemen of the Jury, and all the rest of you wankers out there, here ah ahm, the animal, wae a great big lawbook in ma hand an thinking.

The animal is thinking. He's beginning tae figure it out. Whit yir legal racket's aw about, he's sussed it.

So ah thoat ah wus a fly-boy. Ah thoat ah wus hard. But you loat take the biscuit. Yae beat the band. You've goat the biggest racket of aw and you're the coolest customers because you're legal—and ahm no?

Ah huvnae done any more than the rest o you ur daein every livin day o your free lifes, you're just a bit mair lang-distance aboot it, yae've goat a wee bit finesse—but everything you've goat depends oan thievin and killin o one kind or another—the only difference is that you make the Laws!

But remember this, the animal is thinking.

MOCHAN *has been standing, leaning on his brush and watching* BYRNE *throughout the speech.*

MOCHAN Oh, my Goad, son, yir like a wild stallion wae a man oan its back. Why don't yae just give up an' gie yirsel peace? Yir an awfae hard man.

To audience But he was never hard enough because he couldnae keep control o himself. He suffered frae frustration. He hud aw this energy bilin up inside him an he couldnae get it oot. So there would always come a moment when he wid snap an it wid come oot o him like a torrent. An that wus his undoin. Fur aw that he wus thinkin, he felt too much, an' he let his feelins run away wae him.

It wus because o that he never actually goat tae make his appeal as you'll see in a minit. The famous story ah'm sure you've never heard aboot—"Johnny Byrne Meets the Commando" better unknown as brawn beats its brains oot agen—

Exits with brush

Attention returns to BYRNE

51

Enter Second Prison Officer, RENFREW, *closely followed by* The Commando *who is Assistant Governor of the prison*

RENFREW OK, Byrne. Oan yir feet. The Assistant Governor's here tae see yae.

BYRNE The Assistant Governor. What's he wanting?

RENFREW Don't be impudent. Get on your feet.

BYRNE Just a minute. Who do you think you're talking to?

COMMANDO OK, Renfrew, outside. I'll deal with this alone.

RENFREW Are you sure, sir?

RENFREW I'll be right outside, sir.

BYRNE Yes, sir. No, sir. Three bags full, sir.

COMMANDO You wanted to see me, Byrne.

BYRNE Ah don't, what gives you that impression. I could think o nicer sights.

COMMANDO Don't smart-talk me, Byrne. You've been demanding to see someone for the last ten days.

BYRNE Aye, that's right. Ah think it wis ten days. Might huv been eleven. Ah'm no sure. You lose track of time in this place. You know whit ah mean? Aye but ah think you're right, now that you come to mention it ah huv been asking tae see someone, but ah widnae huv said ah wus *demanding* anything, and ah don't think the person ah wus asking tae see is you. Ah wanted tae see the guvnor, no his assistant. And by the way, ah'll smart-talk you anytime ah like.

COMMANDO How dare you, Byrne. I won't have talk like this in my prison.

BYRNE Oh, it's your prison, is it? Ah wus beginnin tae wunder who owned it. Ah knew it certainly didnae belang tae me. Ah wid huv arranged the furniture different.

COMMANDO You can make things worse for yourself, you know.

BYRNE No much worse, surely.

COMMANDO Yes, but you can make things easy for yourself or you can make them hard, depending on how you behave.

BYRNE Ha! Ha! That's funny. That's ... that's 'rich', as they say, me behave maself ah'm no capable of behavin maself can you people no understand that? Oh, you're a joke so yae ur, comin intae me daein a lifer and telling me tae behave maself. You behave yourself. Awright, so if you've been sent doon tae talk tae the animal yae might as well talk tae the animal. The animal is hoping you have to discuss the witnesses fur its Appeal.

COMMANDO   No, I haven't come here to discuss. I've come here to tell you something. There's nothing to discuss.

BYRNE   Oh? And what is there to tell me?

COMMANDO   You're not going to be allowed to interview the witnesses. Not in this prison. If you want to have witnesses interviewed, you'll have to get a Lawyer to do it for you.

BYRNE   But I'm handling my Appeal myself. I'm entitled to interview witnesses to prepare my case.

COMMANDO   Not if I think there might be a security risk involved.

BYRNE   What?

COMMANDO   I think you heard what I said.

BYRNE   Aye. Ah heard you awright. Ah just couldnae believe what ah wus hearing. Ah don't think you know this, china, but ah know you. You're the wan thae call the Commando. That's the wurd you like tae put aboot this place—that yir wan o the real dirty squad that fought against old Adolf. The Commando. Aye, yir reputations preceded yae.

COMMANDO   And I've dealt with harder men than you, Byrne.

BYRNE   Maybe you have. Maybe yae huvnae.

COMMANDO   But thae never had so much to say for themselves as you seem to have.

BYRNE   You'll have to excuse me. You know, it must've been that life imprisonment sentence the judge passed oan me, it must have give me a shock or something but a strange thing has happened since ah came in here—ah've started thinking. And now that ah've started, ah just cannae seem tae stop. And wan o the things ah've been thinking, it's a funny thing this but I don't really think you think there's a security risk involved at all, you don't seriously think ah wid try tae escape, dae yae? Naw. You're just withholding ma witnesses frae me because *Grabs hold of him* you're so . . . fucking . . . vindictive!

COMMANDO   You let go of me, Byrne.

BYRNE   Naw. Ah'm no letting go o you until you tell me ah'm getting your signature on that piece of paper that ah need!

He is holding THE COMMANDO *with one hand and forming up the other into a clenched fist under his face.* THE COMMANDO *speaks nervously over his shoulder.*

COMMANDO   Renfrew?

BYRNE *finally loses patience and smashes him in the face, snarling with disgust.*

COMMANDO   Officer! Officer! Come quickly!

BYRNE *has let go of him and is laughing happily at the sight of* THE COMMANDO *lying on the floor.* RENFREW *and* JOHNSTONE *run in. They grab* BYRNE *from behind, one on either arm,* BYRNE *is still laughing happily.* THE COMMANDO *gets up and straightens himself out.*

COMMANDO   You'll hear more of this, Byrne.

BYRNE *is still laughing. This next bit, is fast. He breaks in mid-laugh and suddenly he is serious, concentrated. Then he swings up, using the grip of the screws as a lever, taking both feet off the ground and kicking him hard in the groin.* THE COMMANDO *keels over. Grunting with the pain.* RENFREW *leaves go of his grip on* BYRNE *and goes to* COMMANDO'S *assistance.* BYRNE *has relaxed.* JOHNSTONE *keeps a grip on his arm but perhaps it is not so intense as it was a moment before. As* RENFREW *speaks to* JOHNSTONE, *he is bundling* THE COMMANDO *out of the Cell.*

RENFREW   Ah think you'd better lock him up. Ah seem tae remember he's a pal o yours.

JOHNSTONE *locks cell door.* BYRNE *shouts through it, laughing, his hands up at his mouth—cupped.*

BYRNE   *Shouting.* SOME FUCKIN COMMANDO!
His laughter dies away and he is sobbing and gasping. He is desperate and sad. He escapes down the door with his hands, the side of his face pressed against it. He lies on the floor silent, his face resting forehead-down on his arm.

Percussion

MOCHAN   That wus just before ah met up wae him. That wus the beginning o the end wae Byrne and prison. Or maybe you should say

54

the beginning of the ending because it husnae ended yet. Anyway, a strange thing happened in a Glasgow Court following the events just seen. The charge was read out that the accused, John Byrne, had, on such-and-such a day, assaulted a senior prison officer. That wus awright. Nothin unexpected aboot that. Whit wis strange wus the next bit. His lawyer gets up and says:

LEWIS *has walked on during these last words. He delivers his speech formally out to the audience. Immediately after making his speech, he exits. No personal contact is made with audience.*

In behind MOCHAN *and* LEWIS' *speeches,* BYRNE *is set upon by* RENFREW *and* JOHNSTONE *who force him, struggling, into a straight-jacket. Both men are hitting him with batons. Eventually they have him in strait-jacket.* RENFREW *continues hitting him long after might be considered necessary.* JOHNSTONE *restrains him.* BYRNE *is left lying on the stage. The strait-jacket is saturated in blood.*

LEWIS   I am unable to defend my client on this charge because I have not been able to find him. When I went to the prison to prepare his defence, I was told he had been taken away but no-one would tell me where . . .

Exit LEWIS.

MOCHAN   Ah knew where he wus and ah saw the state he came in. He wus in Peterheid and he wus in the solitary block where ah used tae dae some o ma sweeping. And that wus where the real troubles started. Because, among other things, that's where he met a big screw called Paisley. Ah'll tell yae mair aboot him later an ye'll see a wee bit fur yirsel.

BYRNE *is on stage in strait-jacket. He struggles to get out of it. At first there is percussion. Then there is only his voice as a stab against the silence.*

BYRNE   Fuck! Fuck! Fuck! Fuck You!
Fuck You, You Bastards.
Fuck You Fuck You Fuck You.

55

The percussion answers the rhythm. Builds to a crescendo when he bursts the strait-jacket. Then he is on his knees facing the audience. He opens out his arms and roars. He falls slowly backwards, arching himself in a yoga asana. The back of his head (nape of neck) and his heels (soles) touch the floor, but his back is arched between them. What do his arms do? Please see, I. S. Iyengar's "Light on Yoga" for further details. Gradually this can be relaxed. MOCHAN *approaches and looks in at him.* BYRNE *is flat on his back.*

MOCHAN   Johnny Byrne!

BYRNE   Who's there?

MOCHAN   It's Michael Mochan.

BYRNE   Hello there, Michael. Nice tae meet yae. Ah've heard a loat aboot yae. How ur yae daein old-timer?

MOCHAN   Ah'm daein fine. An' what aboot yirsel? An' less o the old-timer.

BYRNE   Ah'm awright. At least ah'm here. Ah've arrived. But it wus a rough journey getting here. Ah think ah'm suffering fae screw-lag. Wid yae mind just telling me where ah ahm?

MOCHAN   Christ, dae yae no even know that? Did they no even tell ye where they were taking yae? You're in Peterheid. Solitary detention wing. Yir no allowed any visitors ur nuthin, so ye'll huv tae make the best o me. Ah'm the only conversation yir gonnae get in here that isnae a crack in the heid. Ah hear yae burst yir straight-jacket.

BYRNE   Ach, it wus weakened. It wus ma ain blood that weakened it. It wus saturated.

MOCHAN   They must huv gied yae some goins over. Wus that done before yae goat here or wus some o it done after?

BYRNE   Some ae it wus here. There's a big bastard aroon here an he wus knockin fuck oot o me. Ah hud tae crack him oan the jaw.

MOCHAN   Did he huv a moustache?

BYRNE   He might huv hud. Ah wusnae really hoping ah'd ever huv tae identify the bastard agen. Aye, but a think he did.

MOCHAN   That sounds like him.

BYRNE   Who in particular?

MOCHAN   Paisley. Some o us caw him the Reverend because he hates aw Catholics. Wae a name like yours, your a gonner. He's a sadistic big bastard. And there's been several cases of brutalisation in this prison because o him in the last two months.

56

BYRNE   Aye. Well ah'm gonnae get tae the governor aboot him.

MOCHAN   He's been had up two or three times but he always gets away wae it. The last time it was fur buggering two of the young prisoners. Everybody knew he'd done it, including his own lawyer, and when he got him off wae it, he wus sick. The lawyer was sick. So there you are, even his own lawyer.

BYRNE   Aye, well let him come for me. I'll be ready for him.

MOCHAN   Did you say you'd cracked his jaw?

BYRNE   That's right.

MOCHAN   Well, don't you worry. He'll be coming for you alright.

Drums. A march. Enter PAISLEY, JOHNSTONE *and* RENFREW. *They face straight on to the audience.* PAISLEY *is one step in front of the other two who form the tips of a triangle behind him. He speaks direct to the audience.*

PAISLEY   I'm Paisley. I'm the one. The bad screw. The one who brings disrepute on all his hard-working colleagues who are making the best of a very tough job. I'm the sadist. The one that's got too much of a taste for the sight of blood. That's what they say. I know it only too well. The prisoners don't like me because they know I don't mess about. I believe in discipline and I believe in using hard methods to tame hard men. And the other   *Pause*   screws don't like me because they know I'm the one that does the dirty work for them.

They know what this prison would be like if we didn't get tough from time to time. They don't want to walk in fear of their life from day to day when they're going about their job, any more than you would. So they tolerate me. I'm *their* hard man. And they feel a wee bit guilty about me because I'm an aspect of themselves they don't like to admit to. Just like you should be feeling guilty about us because we're the garbage disposal squad for the social sewage system. You people out there, that's the way it works for you—you've got a crime problem so you just flush it away one thug after another in behind bars and safely locked away. The cistern's clanked and you can think you can leave it floating away from you to the depths of the sea. Well, ah've goat news fur you—its pollution. Yir gonnae huv tae look ut it. Because if yae don't, wun day its gonnae destroy yae. But in the meantime, dirties like me, well, lets just say we're a necessary evil. Very necessary.

BYRNE and MOCHAN   *Together*   Screws! Screws!

On the chant of "Screws Screws" the drums start their march again. The Three SCREWS *march over to* BYRNE's *cell. Drums stop when they are ranged around* BYRNE. *Important that* MOCHAN *observes all that is happening.*

PAISLEY   OK, Byrne. On your feet. You're going for a wee walk.

BYRNE   Where are you taking me?

PAISLEY   For a wash. You stink.

BYRNE   It doesnae take three of you to take me for a wash.

JOHNSTONE   Come on, Johnny, it's OK.

BYRNE   Johnstone! Ur you followin me or somethin?

RENFREW   Come on. Get these on. *Puts on handcuffs.* We'll decide on staffing in this prison, no you.

BYRNE   *To Paisley.* Could ah no be handcuffed tae somebody else? This guy's breath stinks. Ah'm sure you'd be much nicer.

PAISLEY   Cumon, Byrne, get going and keep the mouth shut. You're going to have plenty of chance tae talk. We've goat one or two questions to ask you.

BYRNE   Wait a minute. What's all this about? I might've known you lot wouldnae give a fuck supposin ah never washed fae wan year tae the next.

PAISLEY   *Pushing him.* Cumon, get moving.

BYRNE   Watch it! Paisley. On second thoughts, you stink more than he does.

PAISLEY *threatens him.*

BYRNE   That's right, ya coward. Ah know all about you. You used tae be a hitman fur the moneylender doon the docks. Did yir 'colleagues' know that?

PAISLEY *hits him.* BYRNE *spits at* PAISLEY. PAISLEY *enraged.* JOHNSTONE *restrains him.*

JOHNSTONE   Take it easy.

PAISLEY   Cumon, move him.

Drums. They move Byrne out of cell towards a sink which represents the washroom. As they cross stage to it, BYRNE *is tugging and pulling at the*

58

handcuff which attaches him to RENFREW. *The effect should be comic.*
MOCHAN *follows them across and watches from a concealed position.*

PAISLEY OK, Byrne. Get in there.
BYRNE Ah'm no going in there. No wae the three o you and no
witnesses.

MOCHAN *makes a thumbs-up sign to the audience to let them know he is
keeping an eye on things.*

PAISLEY *Pushing him roughly* Get in!
RENFREW *Who has been pulled off balance by* PAISLEY's *pushing* Hey,
go easy!
BYRNE *Now in wash area.* Aye, you heard whit the man said.
PAISLEY OK, Byrne. We're taking the handcuffs off, but no funny
business. There's a sinkful of water for you tae wash yourself.

The handcuffs are removed. BYRNE *looks at them all as if he might start
some trouble but then he turns away laughing scornfully, as if he has
decided they are not worth the effort. He sits down at the sink and enjoys
the water.*

BYRNE Oh, this is rerr. Ah suppose you thoat animals like me
wouldnae like water. Did yae bring the DDT powder too?
PAISLEY Give him the towel.

JOHNSTONE *gives him a towel which* BYRNE *takes reluctantly.*

BYRNE Is that aw the wash ah'm gonnae get? Fur fuck's sake, ah never
even goat time tae dae behind ma ears. Whit aboot a shave. Surely
youse can run as far as a shave. Or is shaving forbidden too?
PAISLEY You're damn right its forbidden. We know what you do wae a
razor, Byrne. Dry yourself off. Ah've goat some questions tae ask yae.
BYRNE Oh ho! This is when we find out what its all about, eh? *Dries his
face.* OK, fire away. Paisley. I'm intrigued. *Aside to* RENFREW,
quickly. You didnae think ah'd know a word like that, did yae,
Renfrew?
PAISLEY Stoap playing the innocent, Byrne. What's aw this aboot a
prisoner's charter?

59

BYRNE What? A prisoner's charter. Don't ask me, Ian, ah don't know anything aboot anything as intelligent as that. Ah'm an animal.

PAISLEY We've found a copy of it in the main block and we know you're behind it. There's been nothing but trouble since you were brought here.

BYRNE What does it say?

PAISLEY You know fucking well what it says. A more humane system and investigations . . . investigations of brutality in this prison. . .

BYRNE That sounds like interesting reading. Ah wouldnae mind a copy o that if yae can spare wan.

PAISLEY *Threatening* Don't mess with me, Byrne. What's going oan? You'd better tell us or its more than your life's worth.

BYRNE *Thinks about it* Ah'm tellin you nothing.

PAISLEY Awright! Give him a duckin.

They force BYRNE's *head under water. He struggles throughout.*

JOHNSTONE Will we bring him up?

PAISLEY Naw. Keep him down a minute longer. We'll make him talk. Don't you worry.

JOHNSTONE We'd better be careful.

PAISLEY Listen, son. Don't you try tae tell me. How long huv you been in the prison service?

JOHNSTONE Two years.

PAISLEY Aye, well ah'm comin up fur ten years. So you just keep yir mouth shut. *Pause* OK. Let him up . . .

BYRNE *is released from the water. He shakes his head about and starts shouting as he does so, struggling with* RENFREW *and* JOHNSTONE.

BYRNE Fuck you, you homosexual bastard, Paisley, and fuck King Billy!

PAISLEY OK. Give him another ducking.
They hesitate.
Go on, do it. *They do.* Fur fuck sake, do you see whit he's like. Kindness'll get you nowhere wae that yin. OK. Bring him up again.

BYRNE Fuck!

PAISLEY Awright, Byrne. You'd better start talking or you'll go under a third time and this time you won't come back up.

60

BYRNE *looks up at him slowly, thinking things over.*

BYRNE Awright. So what is it you want to know?
PAISLEY There's something being planned. Some kind of unrest among
the men.
BYRNE That's right.
PAISLEY What is it?
BYRNE They're gonnae cut your balls off.

PAISLEY *hits him.*

They're gonnae cut your balls off an' then they're gonnae serve thaim
up tae the governor oan toast.
PAISLEY OK. Put him under again. And this time . . . *they have his
head under water.* This time . . .don't bother . . . tae bring him up!

*In darkness, noise of prison riot begins. Men's voices shouting. Various
sounds emerge clearly from it. "Up on the Roof". Perhaps the Prisoner's
Charter is read out at this point. Last sound to emerge across the crowd
noise is a voice through a public address hailer:*

"If you come down peacefully, with no trouble, there will be no
recriminations . . . I repeat that . . . no recriminations if you come
down peacefully . . ."

BYRNE *is lying on his bunk.* MOCHAN *speaks through to him excitedly.*

MOCHAN Johnny, waken up. Quick. There's a riot. The men ur up oan
the roof an the press and television's here an everything . . .
BYRNE *Groggy* What?
MOCHAN They're demanding an investigation into prison brutality . . .
Oh, ur you awright. Christ, ah thoat they wur gonnae go the whole
way wae yae that time, Johnny. If Paisley hud hud his way, they wid
have, but Johnstone chickened oot o it.
BYRNE Ah must ah blacked out.
MOCHAN You're lucky yir lungs didnae burst.

61

Sound of loudhailer in distance.

BYRNE What's that?

MOCHAN They're bringing them down. They've been telt that if they come doon peacefully there'll be no recriminations against the ringleaders.

BYRNE Thank Christ fur that. They think ah'm the masterplanner. Masturbator's more fucking like it. Shower o wankers!

MOCHAN Sssh! Listen!

Man howling in the distance.

MOCHAN It sounds as if they're bringing thaim up here to the solitary wing.

BYRNE Aye, and that doesnae sound much like "no recriminations". *Man's voice shouting louder.* "They're kicking me, boys. Leave me alane. Ah hud nothin tae dae wae it".

BYRNE So much fur reason. So much fur the peaceful approach. Bastards!

MOCHAN and BYRNE *Together. Banging and making as much noise as possible* Bastards! Bastards! Bastards! Bastards!

Percussion. The March again. Screws enter to BYRNE. BYRNE *immediately on the ready for a fight.*

PAISLEY You've been creating a bit of a din doon here, Byrne. Did yae think we wouldnae hear you?

BYRNE Ah wahntit yae tae hear me because ah could hear whit you were up tae ya dirty swine. You're a pig. A disgusting Protestant pig.

RENFREW Look at him, the animal, ready fur anuther fight.

BYRNE That's right, crabcrutch, ah'm ready fur you enytime.

They pull their batons.

BYRNE Oh, its the big sticks, is it? Gie me wan and ah'll ram it up yir arse.

JOHNSTONE Don't make things worse fur yourself, Johnny.

BYRNE Aw, cumon, less o the old pals act wae that thing in yir haun. Whit's the matter wae you loat enyway? Wull your old ladies no let yae get it in anymore? Is this how yae ease yir frustrations?

PAISLEY *To others* Haud him. *They grab hold of* BYRNE. PAISLEY *speaks to him with the baton held back, viciously ready for action.* I'm going to enjoy this, Byrne. Aye, you're right. It is frustration. There's been a loat o faces ah've wahntit tae punch and couldnae an' a loat of skulls ah've wahntit tae crack—and couldnae. But wae you ah've got a perfect excuse tae let it aw come out . . .

BYRNE *kicks him and at the same time jumps on* RENFREW. *He jabs his fingers repeatedly in* RENFREW'S *eye, finally getting a hold on the eye, straining as if to gouge it out. He is pulled off by* JOHNSTONE *and* PAISLEY *beats him about the head with his baton.* RENFREW *lies howling on the floor, his hand over his injured eye.*

RENFREW Ma eye! Ma eye! What's he done tae ma eye!

PAISLEY Aw shut up. You'll survive. *Kicks* BYRNE *who is unconscious* And so will he. Worst luck. Ah think he'll need tae go tae a special place. A very special place.

JOHNSTONE *He is helping* RENFREW. Listen, Paisley, there's bound to be an inquiry about this. Renfrew's injured.

PAISLEY Yes. You're quite right, Johnstone. There probably will be an inquiry. But that's no gonnae bother us, is it? No unless you start getting loose wae yir tongue.

JOHNSTONE But they'll see the marks on his head.

PAISLEY That's because he fell on the floor, whilst attacking a prison officer, isn't it? You saw it with your own eyes. You did see it, didn't you?

JOHNSTONE . . . Fell on the floor . . . They'll never accept that.

PAISLEY They've accepted it before. Plenty o times. Come on. We'd better get this yin tae a doctor. *To audience.* Listen, if you excuse him *indicates* BYRNE on the grounds that he's a product of this shit-heap system, then you'd better excuse me on the same grounds.

Drums. They exit.

BYRNE *stands up slowly, composes himself, and walks out of cell towards audience. Before he speaks he smiles. He begins his speech by mimicking the upperclass tones of a Judge.*

63

BYRNE   Ladies and Gentlemen of the Jury. In this trial, as in all criminal trials, the Judge and the Jury have different tasks. Your task is, at the end of the day, to bring in a verdict on the Charge on the Indictment before you. *Own voice* The trial wus a farce. Old Mochan got up and did his bit, right enough. He stuck his neck right out and told them the whole story—detail by detail, as he had seen it wae his own eyes. It wus obvious he was telling the truth but that didnae make much difference. *Smiles again. Judge's voice* You must make up your minds on the credibility and reliability of the evidence you have heard. The matter of the verdict, credibility and reliability, which facts are proved, and which not, are matters for you alone . . .

BYRNE *smiles. Next part is done with off-stage voices*

VOICES   What is your verdict?
The verdict is Guilty.
Is that verdict unanimous or by a majority?
It is by a majority.
BYRNE   My lawyer passed me a note. It said "You didn't stand a chance. It was either you or three married men. They didn't dare do otherwise." After that I went on yet another journey.

Enter three SCREWS. *They lay hands on* BYRNE, *handcuffing him. They push him into centre stage and begin to construct the cage around him.* PAISLEY *punctuates the making of the cage with the speech of the prosecuting advocate, which he delivers with great relish.*
PAISLEY   My Lord, I move for sentence. The Accused is 24 years of age and I produce a Schedule of previous convictions, and your Lordship will see that there have been *fifteen* previous convictions dating from when the accused was a juvenile. The initial convictions are of offences of dishonesty. In particular, in 1963, he was sentenced to two years imprisonment for assault to severe injury and assault by stabbing . . . February 1963, sentenced to imprisonment for assaulting the police and attempting to resist arrest. Two years imprisonment in 1965 for assault and again in October 1965. 1967 sentenced to life imprisonment for murder. 1968 another 18 months for assaulting the assistant governor of one of Her Majesty's prisons, and now, here's a wee bit more for you. Tell him, Renfrew!

64

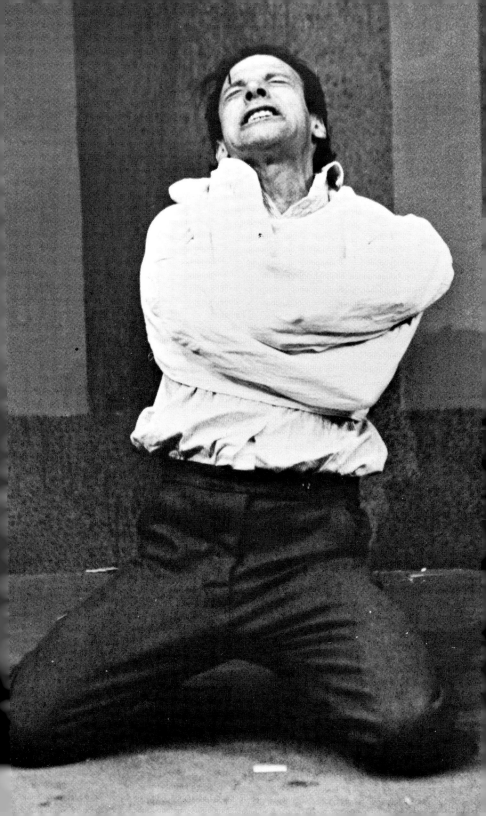

RENFREW *Also taking off Judge* John Byrne. You have a deplorable record and you are now serving a sentence of life imprisonment for murder. *Loud send-up "tut tuts" from* PAISLEY *and* RENFREW I cannot emphasise too much that if you are to serve your sentence of imprisonment in such a way as to obtain some remission, you must behave yourself. PAISLEY *and* RENFREW *nod sagely at this.*

PAISLEY Did you hear that, Johnny? Behave yourself.

RENFREW The sentence I am about to pronounce will have some effect—*laughing in his own voice* you bet your fucking life it'll have some effect—*Judge's voice again* some effect in that it will be taken into consideration if and when you are released,when the time comes for consideration *own voice* but only consideration—of your release. I now sentence you to ha ha ha four years' imprisonment.

PAISLEY Hear that, Johnny? Another four years on top of what you've already got. If you ever get out of here, it will be in your coffin. See you later!

Exit SCREWS.

MOCHAN John Byrne, you've gone beyond the physical wae these people. Its no your body they're trying tae break—its yir proud spirit, because that's what they really fear.

Exit MOCHAN.

Percussion, very quiet and twitchy, behind next sequence. Fluorescent light comes on. It hurts BYRNE's *eyes, his head. He tries to stretch up towards it. Fails. Each time he fails another light comes on. He tries to climb up the bars. Fails. Another light. He crouches, concentrates, prepares to spring. Leaps up, hands stretched out towards light. Falls back on to floor. Another light goes on. Sits with his hands over his eyes. Enter* RENFREW.

RENFREW What's this animal? Going to sleep? Sleeping's not allowed, especially not during the day. Yes, its during the day, animal. I'll bet that surprised you. Never mind. Its nice and bright in here anyway. Isn't it? Look, ah've brought a bit of food for you.

BYRNE *takes his hands from his eyes and looks at food.*

65

E

RENFREW   Hungry, are we, animal? Well, there you are.

Puts plate down outside of bars. BYRNE *tries to reach it with his arm but it is too far away from him.*

RENFREW   Oh, sorry. Can you not reach that? Wait and I'll move a wee
   bit closer for you.

Picks up plate and spits in food. Puts it down within BYRNES *reach.*
BYRNE *looks at* RENFREW, *looks back to food. Stretches his arm
out slowly through the bars, staring at* RENFREW *who moves back a little.
Still staring at him he begins to eat the food—very deliberately—with
his fingers.*

BYRNE   You think you're going to break me, don't you?
RENFREW   *Indicating patch on his eye* Well, you're not exactly my
   favourite person, Byrne, you could say that.
BYRNE   Well, I've got news for you. I've got something in me that can't
   be broken, not by you nor by anybody else—no matter what you do to
   me.
RENFREW   Is that a challenge?
BYRNE   You don't need any challenging. You're going to try it anyway.
   And your food tastes like fucking sawdust. *He throws it out through
   the bars.*

RENFREW *stands up.*

RENFREW   Right, Byrne. That's just what I was waiting for. Paisley!
   Johnstone! *They enter.*
PAISLEY   What is it?
RENFREW   Look at the mess this animal's made. He's getting aggressive
   again.
PAISLEY   Oh well. We'll need to do something about that, won't we?
   Haud yir noses, boys, we're going into his smelly cage . . .

SCREWS *enter cage While* PAISLEY *is talking,* JOHNSTONE *searches with his
hands along top edge of Cage.* RENFREW *holds his nose and looks under
chamber pot.*

PAISLEY   So how do you like your new quarters, Byrne? This is the Cage
and you're in Inverness. Lovely part of the world, Inverness. Too bad
yae cannae get tae see any of it. Aye, yir nice and secure, Byrne.
There's these bars, then there's the four walls round the bars—solid
concrete. Then there's us . . . Awright, get your clothes off.

BYRNE   What is this?

PAISLEY   Get them off or we'll tear them off you.

BYRNE   Come on and try.

JOHNSTONE   We need to search you, Byrne. Official procedure.

BYRNE   Official procedure, my arse. *Pointing at Paisley* It was that
bastard's idea.

Starts taking his clothes off, angrily. When he has stripped BYRNE *places
his hands as a shield for his genitals.*

PAISLEY   OK, search them too. *Referring to clothes.* Right, Byrne.
Stand against the wall. Oh, look at him. Frightened somebody's
gonnae manhandle you, ur yae? Don't worry, we don't want tae know
about your disgusting body. Stand against the wall.

OK Renfrew. Search him. Spread your legs, Byrne.

RENFREW *searches him, looking under his armpits, between his toes,
finally probing his rectum.* BYRNE *reacts violently to this.* RENFREW *gets
away from him fast.*

PAISLEY   Oh, look. He's sensitive.

BYRNE *is looking aggressive.*

PAISLEY   *As they leave the cage* Ah see you've goat that dangerous look
again, Byrne. Well you can save it fur later. We're no quite ready fur
that yet. But we'll be back. Oh aye and ah think we'd better take your
clothes. You never know what mischief he might get tae wae them, do
you lads?

Takes clothes. BYRNE *rushes at them but the cage is locked.*

PAISLEY   Too late, Byrne. Its too late for you for anything. Your time's
up. You've become one of the living dead.

67

BYRNE   No. So long as I'm fighting, I know that I'm alive.

PAISLEY   Aye, well ah've telt yae—we'll be back. And we're gonnae knock the fighting out of your system once and for all.

Drums. Exit SCREWS. PAISLEY *pauses*

PAISLEY   Cover yourself, you disgusting bastard.

BYRNE *makes V signs at* PAISLEY *who laughs. Drums continue. Scotland the Brave.* SCREWS *exit. Starts to pace the interior of the cage. Jogs on the spot. Jogs round the cage. Stops, overcome with weariness for a moment, resting his head against his arm.*

Begins again, doing press-ups and other exercises. Sits down and adopts Yoga half-lotus posture. He feels the floor with the flat of his hand, then runs his hands over the bare skin of his body.

Enter CAROLE. *She stands looking into the Cage.*

CAROLE   Hello, Johnny.

BYRNE   *Putting his hand over his eyes. Turning his head away*   No! No!

CAROLE   Speak to me, Johnny.

BYRNE   *Fist clenched against his brow*   I've got to sleep. Got to sleep.

CAROLE   You can change things, you know, Johnny.

BYRNE   Shut up! Shut up you bloody ghost.

Exit CAROLE. *Enter* KELLY.

KELLY   Hiya, Johnny. Dae yae like ma scar? You gave me it, Johnny. Remember?

Enter DIDI.

DIDI   Aye. Remember, Johnny? Yir Big Brass knew how tae treat yae well. But ah think you've hud yir oats just wance too often.

Enter LEWIS.

LEWIS   There might be a loophole, Johnny, a legal loophole.

CAROLE   Five year six year seven year more.

DIDI   Eight Nine Ten Eleven Twelve Thirteen ... Whit age ur you?

KELLY   They're knockin down the Gorbals. The old place will be gone by the time you get out. If you ever get out.

DIDI   If he ever gets out of here it'll be in his coffin.

Enter PAISLEY.

PAISLEY   Aye. And we'll make sure the lid is well screwed down.

All other characters freeze.

We've come fur yae animal. We've come tae break yae.

BYRNE *stands up.*

BYRNE   Come on then.

Enter JOHNSTONE *and* RENFREW.

BYRNE   Ah promise yae ah'll make it as unpleasant as possible. If yir gonnae break me, yir gonnae break yersels tae. *Laughs* Ah hud a dream under these bright lights, you know, that wis forty winks youse didnae know ah'd hud ...

PAISLEY   *To others.* He's roon the twist. When ah came in he wus talking tae himself and staring like a lunatic.

BYRNE   Ah dreamt ah hud company. A wee fly, buzzing about the place. It came down and landed on ma arm and flew away again. So ah chased after it and ah caught it. Ah watched it buzzing in ma hand for a minit, then a dropt it intae that chanty there. Right intae aw the piss and shit that's all ah've goat left tae show fur ma life. And ah watched it struggle and swim about. Then ah spat oan it. It wus in real trouble then, flailing about. Ah said, Hello there, wee brother. Ah know exactly how you feel. And Ah watched it struggle towards a large lump of shit and crawl up on it for refuge. A moment later ah wus wakened by more of your banging and thumping. And ah could smell your stinking bodies and your smelly feet all the way through those concrete walls. Ah could hear you talking. Ah ran ma hands over ma body and it felt sharp and strong. Ah felt ma own skin and it amazed me.

Ah touched the floor. It was so alive, so *there*. Ah could feel every speck of dust. And when ah looked down, the dust was like jewels, when ah breathed, the air was like nectar. It was strange. Ah felt happy. Ah felt happier than I'd ever felt in my life before. Happy. And grateful. Grateful just to be standing here, breathing in the stinking air. Alive. And ah thought. If that shit could help the fly, it can help me too.

He cakes his body in shit from the chamberpot

So come on. Come on and get me.

Smears over his face

How much of it can you accept?

During this speech the SCREWS *have drawn out their batons. At the end of the speech they have their batons held up menacingly and* BYRNE *stands facing them. At the ready. The lights go down slowly. As they go down, the various characters exit slowly taking off their costumes. The words are delivered wearily and sadly as they exit.*

RENFREW   Rats.
JOHNSTONE   Rats aroon the back.
CAROLE   Rats aroon the back an a wee dug.
PAISLEY   Rats aroon the back an a wee dug that wus rerr ut breakin their necks.
RENFREW   It kilt that many rats it goat a mention in the papers.
CAROLE   It broke that many necks, it goat a medal fur it.
BYRNE   *Lights are almost out.* My name is Byrne, Johnny Byrne. This is my version of my story.

70

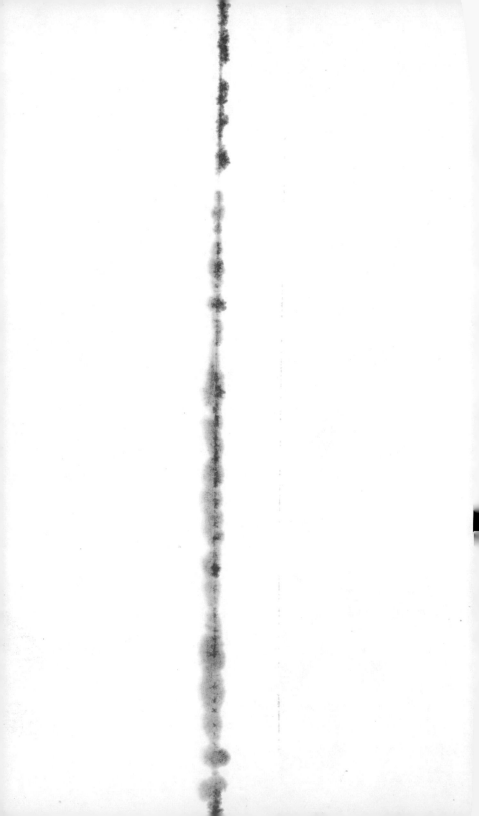

Rawhide Ransom

Cole was a good sheriff, maybe a mite too lenient at times, but when the chips were down, the town of Barberry fully appreciated his prowess with guns and fists.

But they didn't know there was a tragedy in his past that would affect his actions – until a local boy was kidnapped while Cole was supposed to be guarding him. And the only one who could deliver the ransom was Cole himself.

Rawhide Ransom

TYLER HATCH

A Black Horse Western

ROBERT HALE · LONDON

© Tyler Hatch 2009
First published in Great Britain 2009

ISBN 978-0-7090-8743-4

Robert Hale Limited
Clerkenwell House
Clerkenwell Green
London EC1R 0HT

www.halebooks.com

Typeset by
Derek Doyle & Associates, Shaw Heath
Printed and bound in Great Britain by
CPI Antony Rowe, Chippenham and Eastbourne

CHAPTER 1

GUNSMOKE

As the gunsmoke began to clear it revealed the three dead men sprawled in the dirt of Front Street, thin ribbons of blood trickling into the slush of the gutter.

Adam Cole still remained in the half-crouch he had assumed when the gunfight had become inevitable.

'Damn fools. They could still be alive. Jailbait, but breathing.'

No one was close enough to hear his muttered remark. He commenced to reload his Colt. The towns-folk began to appear from their hurried choices of cover when the bullets started to fly; they had huddled in doorways, behind awning posts and rainwater butts, under parked buckboards, some even lying prone in the street itself, having dropped there hurriedly at the first gunshot.

Dusting down their clothes, all of them stared at the lean sheriff as if they had never seen him before.

In a way they hadn't; this man who had cut down three violent bank robbers in their tracks barely resembled the quiet-spoken, non-violent lawman the town council had hired a couple of months ago. He had been popular because he had good manners, raised, or at least touched his hat to the ladies in passing on, the street, settled many an argument by quiet counselling, or just once or twice with his fists. But those times had been few and far between, though once he took on three drunken trail rowdies passing through and ready to hooraw the town. They tried to blind-side him but all three needed attention from Doc Partridge before quitting town, with Cole riding shotgun out as far as the county line.

Folk had wondered about his gun: a used-looking Colt in oiled leather. No one had seen him even brush his hand against the butt and a few worriedly – and quietly – remarked that they wondered how he would react if he *had* to use it.

Now they knew.

The men he had taken on and who now lay dead in the town's main street had been seasoned outlaws, ready and willing to shoot their way out of trouble. They had been led by Louisiana Dann, notorious for his gunplay and violence.

They came running out of the bank, clutching their booty – and stopped dead when they found the lone figure of the sheriff standing there, casually hipshot, hands hanging down at is sides.

'Stop right there, boys, and you'll see sunrise tomorrow.'

6

Startled, they had looked around for this lone lawman's back-up – he surely would have five or six deputies planted somewhere. . . ?

There was no sign of even *one*.

Good enough for Dann. Playing to the staring, nervous townsfolk, he spoke to Cole: 'You're the one ain't gonna see the sunrise!'

People scattered before all the words were spoken and the guns came up blazing.

There was a brief volley of scattered shots and, later, several witnesses maintained that Cole only fired three times – and Louisiana Dann and his pards lay dead in the dust, the stolen moneybags crumpled under their bodies.

And now the dissipating gunsmoke revealed the whole scene and fast-talking townsfolk crowded around.

'He got all three!'

'Never seen him draw!'

'They had him surrounded – the poor bastards!'

'They never stood a chance!'

Cole was jostled, patted on the back, several men insisted on shaking his hand.

'Someone get a door and take 'em down to the undertaker's.' Cole spoke tersely, obviously uncomfortable with all this attention. 'And get that money back in the bank! Every damn cent!'

'I'm taking care of that, Cole. My clerks will see it's all collected.'

Linus Charlton, the town banker, looked sallow, face drawn, although his figure was corpulent enough and normally his face had a florid, pudden-look. He was trying to light a long thin cigar, his hands shaking, the match flame burning his fingers. Cole snapped a vesta on his thumbnail and held it for Charlton.

'Easy, banker. It's all over. Anyone hurt inside?'

'Uh – two clerks, I think. Yes, Ernie Hall and Benton Ness. One female clerk fainted.'

'They need a doctor?'

'Ernie will. They split his scalp and knocked him cold.' Just then Doctor Partridge appeared, hurrying up with satchel in hand, and the banker directed him inside. Then he looked back at Cole; the cigar seemed to have calmed him some but he had an almost angry look on his face.'By God, I – we never expected to see anything like this, Cole!'

'What you hired me for.'

'Yes – and thank God we did hire you. Just three shots and that gang is ready for Boot Hill! How come you never told us how good you were when the committee interviewed you?'

'They asked if I was fast with a gun and I said I'd been fast enough so far.' His deep voice held hardly any interest. He jerked his head at Charlton and walked to the law office on the opposite side of the street, the crowd opening out to let him pass.

He was seated at his desk, rolling a cigarette when the banker puffed in, half-smoked cigar down at his side. He dropped into a chair.

'I think this calls for a drink.'

The sheriff fired up and swung the chair around, bending to open a drawer in the desk. He set a whiskey bottle and two shot glasses on the paper-cluttered top and poured two drinks, filling each glass to the brim.

The banker spilled a lot of his before tossing it down. Cole sipped about half, savouring the taste.

'You seem a bit . . . put out, Cole. Look, don't worry about Dann and his friends. They were scum. They'd killed a lot of people over the years. They're better off dead.'

'Would seem that way.'

Charlton frowned. 'This . . . bother you? Hell, man, your reputation will sky-rocket! You'll be known all over the county, maybe the whole damn state, as the fastest gun ever to come—' He stopped abruptly at the look on Cole's face. 'Is that what's bothering you? Word'll get out about your gunspeed and. . . .'

Cole savagely crushed out his barely smoked cigarette in the old coffee-can lid, grey-blue eyes pinched down and cold.

'That's exactly what bothers me, banker! Every goddamn rowdie from here to hell – and back – will show up and want to try my speed!'

'Well, I doubt any of 'em'll be faster than you! Why, the way you got that Colt out . . . My God! This has happened to you before, hasn't it?' Cole stared bleakly. 'But I don't recall the name. . . .'

'Different from the one I'm using now. You wouldn't know it if you heard it.' The sheriff shook his head sharply. 'Damn! I should've known better, should never've taken this job. But I was broke and you offered good pay and – and this is a *quiet* town! Out of the way of the cattle trails, stage-run once a week, a few drunks

9

on Saturday night, no wild-whooping trail hands wanting to lift the roof!' He tightened his lips. 'Then this . . .
situation arises and there was only one way to settle it!'

'And you sure did that!'

Cole slammed his hand down flatly on the top of the
desk, the concussion overturning the empty shot glasses
and spilling a few papers to the floor, where they lay
ignored.

The banker looked uneasy. 'Er – Cole, I sure as hell
hope this isn't going to . . . influence you, whether you
stay on or not! I know you were on a three-month trial,
but, man, we can't afford to lose you! It might be once
in a blue moon when something like today happens,
but, by God, when it does, you're the kind of man we
want to see behind that badge! Please – and I know I
speak for the whole town when I say this – *please* don't
even think of quitting! I believe I have enough authority with the selection committee to promise to lift your
wage, or maybe present you with a cash token of the
town's appreciation. Would you consider those things?'

Cole didn't answer right away. 'Money's not my main
interest. I've earned enough for my present needs. It
could take me a long way from here.'

The banker was alarmed. 'Oh, now, listen, Cole!
Don't make any rash decisions! You go back to your
hotel room and relax, think about things.' He lowered
his voice. 'There's one real nice young woman down the
trail at Banjo Springs. No trouble to send for her. Name
of Willow.' He winked and half-smiled. 'And that's
appropriate! She clings like a willow but I've never
heard her weep yet. Sometimes moan, though, and—'

'Go fix your bank, Linus,' Cole interrupted. 'I don't need any female diversions, or the other kind that comes out of a bottle. I'll think about things and let you know come morning.'

It was flat and final and the banker stood slowly, nodding jerkily.

'All right. But I hope you make the right decision, Cole! It could be a lot more serious than you think.'

The sheriff frowned slightly. Did he imagine it or was there a hint of threat in the banker's words. . . ?

'You like to explain that?'

Linus Charlton waved a hand, a little thrown off his stride now as those chilly eyes bored into him. 'I mean, the effect it's going to have on the town if you decide to move on. It doesn't bear thinking about.'

Cole held the man's gaze a moment longer and said heavily, 'Mebbe I'm tired of moving on, Linus. Hell, no "mebbe" about it! I've done a lot of it and I really thought I'd found a place here where I could live quietly. You've no idea how disappointed I feel right now.'

The banker's face softened. 'You sure never hesitated to tackle those robbers!'

'I took your money,' was Cole's only comment.

The banker suddenly held out one of his pinkish, uncalloused hands. Cole was surprised but gripped it briefly.

'Stay, Cole. Stay with us. There'll be more money whatever happens, and if there's something else you want as part of the deal – well, you just speak up. And if we can get it for you, it's yours.'

11

Adam Cole watched him cross the street through the dusty window. There was still a crowd outside the bank, studying the ground where the robbers had fallen.

You can't give me what I want, Banker. No one can.

CHAPTER 2

TROUBLES

There was a kind of delegation and it immediately made Cole edgy. He saw them coming through the law office window, a bunch of the town's businessmen – all members of the select committee – heading his way.

He swore and put away the whiskey bottle; he didn't aim to offer his good booze to this lot. By then they were coming in the door, led by the smiling banker.

'As promised, Cole,' Charlton said, adding a belly laugh for no good reason the sheriff could see. The banker gestured to a man in a frayed frock-coat and a white shirt spotted with food droppings. This was Miles Burnside, the town's only lawyer, still a bachelor and heading fast for sixty years old come December.

He had a small leather valise and opened it, taking out a long manila envelope. Cole saw that his name had been written on it in Burnside's famous Olde English style lettering. The lawyer cleared his throat and held out the envelope.

'On behalf of the good citizens of Barberry, all seven hundred and forty-three—'

'Forty-four, Counsellor,' interrupted Griff Cavanaugh who ran the general store. 'Mrs Grandison whelped another daughter just before breakfast. Doc Partridge sent for a bunch of clean towels, and luckily I'd just gotten in a shipment from—'

Burnside frowned. 'I stand corrected then. Well, adding Mrs Grandison's as yet unnamed daughter to the population, we are happy to present you with this token of our appreciation for saving our money, which was being stolen by the now deceased, Louisiana Dann gang.'

There was a county cheque inside the envelope made out to Adam Cole for the sum of $2,000. His eyes widened a little as he read and Banker Charlton said quickly.

'We trust it will be sufficient for your wants, Cole – but not enough to take you away from our town.'

Cole looked up amd smiled thinly. 'Gents, I do believe I'm being bribed – and that's agin the law.'

The delegation's faces straightened and they all looked at Counsellor Burnside.

He cleared his throat. 'It would only be against the law if you were our duly elected sheriff, Cole. As you are still on probation, as it were, you may accept our offering with a clear conscience – and right after, we can declare you Barberry's official new sheriff, with increased salary. Amount to be determined by negotiation, plus privileges.'

Cole's expression didn't change as he studied the cheque. Then he looked up, smiling all the way this time.

'I thank you gents. I just happen to have a newly polished sheriff's star in my top drawer.'

They laughed as he brought out the badge. The tip of one arm of the star was slightly bent from the accident that had killed the previous sheriff. Emerson, the undertaker and church deacon, said in his usual sin-killing voice, the loudest and most resonant in town,

'I b'lieve we might've saved some money, gentlemen! Seems to me this probationary lawman was plannin' to stay on as sheriff all along.'

That started more laughter and Cole relented. He brought out his whiskey bottle but was short of glasses.

'Fill the ones you've got,' suggested Griff Cavanaugh, 'and pass the bottle round. We ain't too proud to drink our whiskey direct.'

There was unanimous agreement and Mannering, who ran the town's only saloon, went away and came back with six extra glasses and two more bottles of whiskey.

It was just as well no one broke the law in town that afternoon or evening – and part of the night. . . .

When they at last decided to leave – two wives had arrived and had stood on the law office porch, berating their now very merry husbands, breaking up the revelry – only Banker Charlton remained. Cole sat down again in his chair, wiped his sweating face and loosened his trouser belt.

'That was . . . pleasant, Linus. Kind of thing I've been

looking for. Guess I have you to thank you for it, the money and so on—'

'Not at all. Thank yourself for stopping the robbery. They'd almost cleared out the safe. A *lot* of money would have been missing and a lot of folk would have suffered because of it.'

Cole shrugged. 'Well, the only thing I can add is that I'll give the job a try for a couple of months and—'

Charlton sobered. 'We intend for you to stay in the job a lot longer than that, Cole!'

The sheriff, now wearing the damaged star on his shirt, held up a hand. 'Told you I was looking for somewhere I could settle in peace and quiet, Linus. Reckon there's a good chance of me finding it here. Like you say, that robbery attempt by Dann was unusual, but if it brings in a lot of fellers wanting to try my gun speed . . .' He shook his head briefly, 'I'll just have to move on.'

'Well, I'll pass this along to the committee, Cole, but it's not what we expected.'

'If you want the cheque back, that's OK. Like Burnside said, I had decided to stay on, but only for a spell, a trial period.'

'Keep the money. Our appreciation of what you did isn't in any way lessened, but we would like to see you as our *permanent* sheriff.'

'Let's see how things work out, Linus.' He wiped a hand across his face. 'Whew! I like the odd snort but I'm glad we don't have a session like this every night.'

Banker Charlton smiled. He, too, was feeling the effects of the whiskey. He glanced at his gold pocket watch and heaved to his feet.

'I sure as hell better be going. Bess will be blowing steam out of her ears by now. My dinner will be either burned or cold – or maybe the dog got lucky!'

They laughed and Cole closed the door behind him, turned the key in the lock and leaned against the paint-peeling wood. His tired eyes travelled slowly around the lamp-lit office.

Well, you could've said "no, thanks". Now you're stuck here for at least a couple of months. He glanced at the tattered calendar on the wall. His gaze went immediately to July 7 – a Friday, just under four weeks away. He felt his belly knot. Damn fool! You should've made that a one-month trial, not two. Now you'll be here when it comes around – the first time in five years you haven't passed that day – and *night* – alone, in some isolated place with just the stars and the wilderness and no one to see, or hear, but you, your horse and God – if he's anywhere around!'

He glanced at the whiskey bottle on the desk. There was a good inch remaining in the bottom.

He snatched it up and drained it, then groped his way to his chair, slumped into it and drifted away into a disturbed sleep.

Bess Charlton was Linus's second wife. As well as a deal of property and cash left by her deceased first husband, she had brought to the marriage, Donny, her eight-year-old son. As far as Linus was concerned the kid was the biggest pain in the butt he had experienced since an acute attack of the piles.

17

Probably Donny was no better or worse than the average eight-year-old, but there was instant hostility between him and Banker Charlton. Donny didn't even like the name and tried to keep his original one: Curtis.

Bess wouldn't hear of it. 'I'm marrying Linus Charlton, Donny, and that's the name I will take. You are my flesh and blood, so you will now become Donny Charlton. I'll have no argument! That's it!'

Bess was a woman used to having her own way and one time, in a fit of pique, Donny had told her this, adding that she had been 'spoiled' by Lawrence Curtis. It was the last time Donny sassed his mother about that.

But he turned his juvenile anger and frustration towards Charlton, who was not much good with children anyway.

'You're not my father!' Donny often used this statement of truth when Charlton hardened his voice and tried to exert authority over the boy for one reason or another. 'I don't like you!'

'Mutual, my dear stepson, I assure you. It's *mutual*!' He looked around swiftly, lowered his voice, his tone not changing. 'And you keep up this insolence and you'll be eating like a horse for a week – *standing up*!'

Donny curled a lip, showing his small white teeth. 'You're not funny! Except for the way you look! Like a ball with a turnip on top!'

Linus almost ruptured himself in exerting the force he put behind the kick he aimed at the darting boy. He missed, of course, and so the effort strained his groin even more. Gasping, clutching his side low down, he managed a curse.

'I'll fix your wagon ... one of these days, kid! You can count on it!'

Donny pressed a thumb to his upturned, freckled nose and waved all four fingers in the current ultimate insulting gesture at the small Barberry school.

Bess was aware that the relations between her new husband and her eight-year-old were dismal and after a while she gave up trying to improve them. Sometimes – most times – she took the boy's part anyway and this made her own relations with Linus less than sweet and wonderful.

But they survived and they lived very well, probably better than anyone else in Barberry. This was in part due to Linus's good salary from the Frontier First National Bank. He was paid well to manage this out-of-the-way branch in a small town like Barberry. The lifestyle was occasionally given a lift by Bess's own contribution from money left to her by her dead husband. *Only occasionally.*

By the accepted and unwritten law of the day, her bank balance and property holdings were supposed to be accessible to Linus at any time. But when he first made her aware of this, she placed a hand on one of her ample hips, narrowed those icy-blue eyes and shook her blond head.

'No, Linus. Curtis earned this money and invested wisely. It has nothing to do with you. It was all for the benefit of Donny and myself. I believe you will find me generous on occasion, but it will be at my option.' Then she smiled that devilish smile that got him all heated and short of breath. 'And I haven't heard any

19

complaints from you when I have felt generous with my . . . favours in the past.' She laughed lightly at the flushed look a his face, knew why he was squirming.

He swallowed, nodded, drew out a kerchief and mopped his heated face swiftly. 'As you will, my dear. After all, it's your money. . . .'

But he would love to get his hands on some of it! Deuce Mannering ran such marvellous card games in the rear of his saloon, late at night. . . ! If he could only match some of the bets made by these visiting ranch owners from the neighbouring county whom he invited to the game!

Cards and dice had always thrilled him; once he lost an appointment in a Missouri bank because of his liking for gambling. 'Not appropriate for a bank manager, Mr Charlton. Sorry.'

Still, lately he had done all right with a little manip-ulation, which no one had detected or even known about, let alone Bess.

But there was some pressure on him by Mannering, who actually worked for the big saloon owners in Banjo Springs. They called their gaming rooms (legal in Banjo County) casinos – a foreign word, but with a wonderful sound to it, like cards slithering and dice rattling.

The first fast gun arrived in town on the second stage after the thwarted bank robbery. A little under two weeks.

He didn't look very different from the cowboys and drifters who passed through the town. He wore range clothes that had seen better days, a leather vest with a tobacco-sack tag dangling from the left upper pocket, a single gunbelt and holstered Colt, scuffed riding boots, tarnished spurs.

He swung a warbag casually over his shoulder and stopped a depot clerk, easing back his curlbrim hat from his face.

'Friend, can you point me in the direction of the law office?'

'Why, sure. Turn left at the gate and end of the lane is Front Street. Left again and it's about halfway along.' The clerk, young and impressionable, added, 'Er . . . You heard about our Sheriff Cole? An' how he stopped the Louisiana Dann gang dead when they tried to rob our bank?' He winked. 'An' I mean *stopped 'em dead*!'

The cowboy nodded slightly, smiled; he had a pleasant enough face, hard-jawed, but maybe the eyes had a mean look to them. 'B'lieve I did hear somethin'. Fluke, weren't it?'

'Fluke? Like hell! If you'd seen Cole move – well, you wouldn't've. No one seen him draw. Just his gun was suddenly there in his hand, blazin', and them three robbers were down in the dust. Not even kickin' they died so fast.'

The cowboy's smile had disappeared now. 'No one's that fast! Not even Hickok.'

'I dunno 'bout that. Mr Hickcok ain't never been to this town, but I sure wouldn't care to go up agin Sheriff Cole—' He stopped suddenly, looked sharply at the man, noting now that the base of the holster, worn quite low on the thigh, was tied down with a rawhide thong. The leather had been cut away around the trigger guard to allow swifter access for the finger and . . . The clerk swallowed. 'I – I best get on with my work, mister. Just do what I said and you'll find the law office. All right?'

'Yeah, sure. Thanks, friend.'

He flipped a quarter and the clerk deftly caught it. He watched the man stroll up the lane, the warbag slung over his shoulder – his *left* shoulder he now noticed, keeping his gun arm swinging free.

He hurried back into the depot, calling to one of the drivers who was filling out his usual papers:

'Zeke! I . . . I think there's gonna be another shootin'.'

Cole was seated at his desk, writing up some reports for the town council when a shadow darkened his doorway. The dusty cowboy stood there, framed by the bright sunlight from the street, no more than a blurred outline to the sheriff.

Recognizing the ploy, Cole was immediately alert and laid down his pen. 'Come on in.'

'I'll do my talkin' from here.'

Cole nodded and thrust slowly to his feet. 'Then I better come across and get a look at you.'

As he stepped around the desk and approached the doorway the man smiled crookedly. 'They call me Flash Jack Cotton.'

Cole stopped, leaning one hand on the edge of the door. He nodded. 'Expected you earlier.'

Cotton blinked. 'You don't know me!'

'And don't want to. But you're no different from any other two-bit *pistolero* who figures he's the fastest gun alive and aims to prove it by outdrawing me.'

Cotton smiled again. 'You're lookin' right at him, Cole. Make it good, 'cause I'm gonna be the last thing you ever see.'

'Getting right down to it, huh?' Cole sighed. 'Well, guess that's the best way. OK. Let's get it done.'

Then he slammed the door closed and heard the muffled cry of agony through the heavy woodwork and the clatter as Cotton was smashed back against the porch rail. It gave way and the cowboy sprawled on his back in the street, warbag flying into the slush of the gutter.

By that time Cole was standing on the landing, looking down at the man who now had a bloody face and was struggling to stand. Cole held up a hand – his left. 'Be wise to stay put, friend. Unless you're gonna make a run for the depot. You'll just about make the stage turn-around.'

Flash Jack Cotton had other ideas, as Cole knew he would; the man hadn't come all this way to be knocked down by a swinging door. He thrust to his feet, stooped over and half-turned towards Cole as if making an effort to push upright. Instead, his Colt left leather with a deadly whisper and flame spurted from the barrel as he spun, fully facing Cole now.

Not for long. Cole's lead took him in the crook of his gun arm and he screamed as he floundered back, his arm jerking violently, bone splinters tearing through the bloody flesh. Cotton's smoking Colt spun from his fingers, which could no longer hold its weight.

And never would again.

A crowd gathered in moments, folk running up from all directions. Cole picked out the sweating stage clerk.

'Billy, have someone help you get him to Doc Partridge. This fool's got money jangling in his pocket so he can pay for whatever attention Doc gives him. Put the rest towards a stage ticket back to Banjo Springs – or as far as it'll take him.' He swung his bleak gaze to the writhing, sobbing would-be gunfighter. 'He won't be coming back to this town.'

CHAPTER 3

ULTIMATUMS

Ten days later the second challenger arrived, coming in from the north.

He rode a dust-spattered paint with a sidekick forking a shaggy roan alongside. The one who turned out to be the challenger was a small man, no more than five feet four or five. He wore two guns on a *buscadero* rig with plenty of fancy carving in the leatherwork. *Spanish*, most folk said, recognizing the style as coming from below the Border.

Someone with better eyes than the others and more knowledge of guns pointed out that the Colts' handles had been shaved down to allow a better fit in the man's small hands.

The men rode straight past the law office, not even glancing in its direction, and dismounted outside Mannering's Delta saloon.

Inside they ordered whiskey and the taller one pushed a coin towards the barkeep from the change pile.

'Have one yourself.'

'Thanks, *amigo*, but boss don't allow it. You boys from up north?'

'What makes you say that?' demanded the small man, sounding irritated.

'That yaller dust all over you. Has to be from the Canary Desert.'

'Everyone a smart-ass in this town or just you?' the aggressive man cracked. The barkeep straightened and moved away down the counter. The small man slapped a hand down hard on the scarred woodwork. 'Hey, you! I asked you a question!'

The tall man placed a hand on the other's arm. 'Easy, Frankie, we don't need trouble here.'

'Why not? It'll bring Cole, won't it?'

'That ain't how we planned it!'

'Trouble with you, Biff, you're bigger'n me but your brain's smaller. You can't adapt to a change in plans.' And as he spoke he whipped up one of his guns, the left one, and shot out the bar mirror. Glass and bottles leapt in a wild cascade, cutting the cringing barkeep. The man held a grey bar towel to his bleeding face.

'The hell you doin'?'

'Gettin' your attention – or your sheriff's. If he ain't too busy, or somethin', to come see what's happenin'.'

Biff groaned, seeing it was way too late to stop his smaller pard now.

'You might be sorry if Cole does come!'

The barkeep yelped and jumped as Frankie fired over the counter, his bullet taking the already bleeding man in the foot. He collapsed, gritting his teeth, stifling

26

a howl of pain.

Mannering, watching from his office doorway, spoke quietly over his shoulder to someone behind him. 'Go get Cole.'

'No need, boss.' A hand came over Mannering's shoulder, pointing in the direction of the batwings which had just slapped back. Cole entered, gun still in holster, but eyes darting around the smoke-dimmed room, his body tense, his movements catlike and alert.

He soon saw the source of the trouble, and identified it immediately as Frankie bared his teeth, holstering his six-gun.

'Biff, I b'lieve we are now honoured with the presence of Sheriff Adam Cole, self-styled fastest gun alive – the poor bastard!'

'You're Frankie Delgado.'

'Glad you recognize me.' The pigeon chest puffed out some.

'Saw you once in Fort Griffin. You shot a half-drunk buffalo runner, wounded him, made him crawl along the street and howl like a dog, shooting at him all the time. Till you finished him off. Thing is, one of those bullets ricocheted and killed a lady on a hotel balcony, knitting a shawl for the baby she hoped to have in a few weeks.'

Delgado wasn't pleased at the accusation but didn't deny it. 'Main thing was, you seen how fast I am. That buff-runner was really Hi-Spade Hunnicutt, hidin'-out after killin' a man in El Paso. Man he killed was a pard of mine. Hi-Spade deserved to die.'

'The pregnant woman didn't.'

27

Delgado sobered, then shrugged. 'OK, you wanna make that the excuse to try to take me in,'s OK by me.' He set his short legs firmly and the crowd pressed back – but not too far. Everyone wanted to see this. 'But I ain't goin' with you!'

Biff leaned against the bar after moving along a little way, putting some distance between Frankie Delgado and himself. But just far enough along so that he was slightly to the rear of the sheriff, who hadn't taken his eyes off the small man.

'Guess you're not too confident, Frankie. Having Biff there ready to cover you in case you're not as fast as you figure.'

Delgado looked fit to bust. 'The hell I ain't!'

And that was it: no more talk. It was put up or shut up time.

He was damned near as fast as he believed. Frankie's guns seemed to snap into line with his hands braced against his small hips as they blazed.

Cole staggered even as he fired. One shot. It almost took Delgado's head off, snapping it back as if his neck was made of wet cardboard. The impact lifted his small feet from the sawdusted floor, hurling his body against the bar. He was still falling towards the floor when Biff triggered and Cole's second bullet took him through the heart.

And, to the surprise and consternation of the drinkers, their sheriff was down on one knee, head hanging, gun hand on the floor, the arm supporting his weight.

*

28

A few weeks after the bank robbery attempt, Bess floored Linus with her announcement over dinner:

'I'm thinking of taking a trip to the West Coast, Linus. I know you can't get away from the bank at this time of year, so it will be just Donny and me. It's time he met his Uncle Carl.'

Charlton almost choked on the last boiled potato and had to snatch at the water jug to fill his glass, but Donny, with an innocent smile, reached the jug first. He not only pulled it quickly towards him but knocked it over, spilling its contents.

'Gee, Linus,' he refused to call him 'Dad' or 'Father', even 'Pop' – 'I'm sorry. I – I'll go pump some more in a minute and fill the jug. You be OK till I get back? I mean, I wouldn't want you to choke or anything—'

'Donny!' shouted Bess, half-rising, eyes narrowed. 'Get through to the kitchen and pump that water! Hurry, you little devil!' She lunged towards her gagging husband and clapped him between the shoulders as Donny strolled towards the kitchen doorway.

'*Move*, damn you!' It was the first time Linus had heard her use a cuss-word and Donny sure looked surprised. He started to run.

After Linus had settled down and was massaging his flabby throat, she made the boy apologize, which Donny did – with the worst possible grace. He was sent to bed without any more supper, but Linus knew she would sneak him a piece of pie or some kind of sweet-meat later.

'So. You've timed your holiday to coincide with the busiest part of the year for my bank! The land sales,

29

reassessment of mortgages, my inspection of outlying farms we have loaned money on—'

'I'm sorry, dear. You know I'm impulsive, and once I get an idea in my head—'

'Oh, yes! I know, all right! But dammit, Bess, I'd love to see San Francisco.' They had great gambling halls there, he had been told, the stakes sky-high: why, some of the richest land-and-cattle owners in the US had gotten their start in the 'Frisco gaming halls.

'Well, it'll be better if we go now, before Donny starts the more serious side of his education. I wouldn't want to interrupt his schooling.'

'Oh, goodness, *no*! That would be unthinkable. How long do you estimate to be away?'

'I haven't given it much thought – a few weeks, I daresay. I might even spend the winter there. Carl says it's much milder and there are no blizzards like the ones that sweep this God-forsaken hole. . . .'

'Months! And what the hell am I going to do? Who's going to keep house for me? Make my meals, wash my clothes. . . ?'

Of course, Bess didn't do those things now: they had a live-in cook and maid-of-all-work, and Bess coolly reminded him of that now. 'You'll be well looked after, Linus, dear.'

'Your mind's made up, I see.'

'Yes. It just . . . came to me. All detailed and everything. I need some decent clothes. I'm sick of mail order and never getting exactly what I expect. Curtis sent me to New York once, and Philadelphia and it was marvellous. I will, naturally, use my own money. You won't be out of pocket.'

'I would not expect to be! Damnit, Bess, Curtis didn't have the responsibility of running a bank!' growled Linus, knowing it was no use throwing one of his tantrums: she was too damn hard for that to work. 'He could afford to pamper you and. . . .' He let the words trail off. What was the use? She was immovable.

But, by God, he would throw a spanner in the works if he could. Just the thought of that smirking little swine enjoying the sights of an exciting town like 'Frisco while he slaved away at all the problems this time of year seemed to magnify. . . !

'I'm going for a walk,' he announced abruptly.

'Would you like my company, dear?' Bess asked sweetly. 'It's a balmy might and—'

'My own company is all I can stand right now!'

'Of course, dear. I agree wholeheartedly.'

He grunted as he jammed on his hat and strode angrily out into the night.

He hadn't gone half a block before he stopped dead on the boardwalk.

My God! That sneaky damn Jezebel! Curtis's brother, Carl was a lawyer and executor of his brother's will. He took care of the estate, advised Bess how she should spend or invest her money. Audited the books. . . .

He knew she had received a letter from Carl a couple of weeks ago. Now she had *impulsively* decided to make the long, arduous trip to California, taking Donny with her. That part was OK, but why was she going now and what was she taking with her?

'Oh, blast!' Linus hissed, unaware of the beauty of

the star-studded evening and a couple of passers-by wishing him 'Good night'.

He felt sick to his stomach.

He turned and hurried back towards the large house on the hill at the end of Lavender Street.

He had just remembered he had left the keys to the house safe on his bedside table; there were things in there she shouldn't see!

Linus began to run.

CHAPTER 4

INDEPENDENCE DAY

Cole had set up a chair with footrest on the Front Street balcony of the Star Hotel where he had booked a room after receiving his 'appreciation bonus' from the town committee. Prior to that, he had slept in the small room out back of the law office, even, on one occasion, spent a night in one of the cells, trying out the bunks: no feather bed.

Now he figured he could afford a little luxury so why not enjoy it?

The footrest had been designed by Doc Partridge and consisted of cushions placed in the top part of two crosspieces of wood forming two 'Xs' and connected by slats of timber. It formed a kind of cup and supported Cole's foot and lower leg. And he needed it; Delgado's bullet had creased his left hip and it still hurt enough after a couple of weeks for him to have to use a stick when getting around.

At least there had been no more challengers since Delgado and Biff had taken up residence in the Barberry Boot Hill. He had decided that if any more drifters came in and wanted to test his gun speed, he would pull up stakes. He was reluctant to do that, because he liked Barberry and its folk. It was a town that would have a good future when this part of the country was opened up by more railroads; but he would probably move out before then.

He was a small-town man, always had been. Luckily, Alice had shared his liking for such places and if things had been different. . . .

He reined in his thoughts right there. Nothing could change it now so what was the point in thinking about it?

But he knew the present date, July 1, and that meant the time he dreaded was drawing close. Not the Fourth, with its planned celebrations, but the Seventh, which had a different kind of meaning for him.

'How's the leg, Cole?'

He started a little at the enquiring voice, hitched around and saw Banker Charlton coming towards him along the balcony. The man's left hand was heavily bandaged and he held it level across his waist as if to ease its discomfort.

Cole stared at it as he answered slowly, 'Gonna throw away this damn stick in another day, whether I fall flat on my face or not.'

Linus smiled, sat down in a wicker chair and lit one of his cigars, awkwardly, mostly using his right hand and the two unbandaged fingers. He offered the case to Cole, who shook his head and rolled a cigarette.

'What happened to your hand?'

The banker waved his cigar, trying to be casual but there was tension there and an abruptness to his words that made it clear he didn't want to discuss it in detail.

'Tripped on one of Bess's confounded mail-order floor rugs in my office. Put my hands out to save myself and cracked a couple of fingers. Painful but more of a nuisance than anything.' He drew quickly on his cigar and exhaled the smoke, speaking as he did so. 'The committee's arranged for the Miller brothers to be on call if you need them to lend a hand on the Fourth's celebrations. Satisfactory, Cole?'

Cole nodded curtly. 'Hope they won't be needed.'

'We-ell, it *is* Independence Day. Folk might get carried away some. Kids are always a bit of a problem, letting off fireworks with no thought of where they light them or where they might land.'

Cole's face suddenly straightened out. 'If kids are the biggest problem, that'll suit me,' he said curtly. 'With all that home-brewed rotgut being handed round, though, there's going to be a slew of drunks.'

Charlton frowned. 'Well, folk have to let their hair down now and again. Er – can I ask you a favour? Keep a special eye on young Donny? He's an irritating kid and I confess I don't get along too well with him, but – well, he's Bess's son and I wouldn't want any real harm to come to him.'

'Just a little harm'll be OK, though, eh?'

Linus blinked, sat up straighter. 'I didn't mean it that

way! I – Oh! You're joshing me.'

'Trying to. That's how bored I am, Linus, amusing myself with feeble jokes.'

'Once you get back onto your feet and have a few celebratory drinks on the Fourth, you'll perk up. Will you watch out for Donny?'

For a moment the banker thought the sheriff was going to refuse, but he nodded jerkily. 'Sure. But I guess I'll have plenty to do so don't expect me to follow him around and wipe his nose for him.'

'Of course not. He can wipe his own nose, anyway. But he admires you, like all the kids in town, following you around, playing "Sheriff Cole" with wooden guns and so on. I'll be obliged, Cole.'

'I'll see he doesn't get into any trouble.' Struggling some, Cole got his stick and used it to lever himself out of the chair, putting his left foot down gingerly, transferring the weight a little at a time. 'Ah! Feels better than it did yesterday. Think I'm getting there, Linus.'

He leaned on the stick, looking steadily at the banker's bandaged hand, then lifted his gaze to Linus's face. The man seemed uncomfortable under that stare. 'Haven't had much to do except sit up here and watch the street and passing parade for a few days, Linus.' The hard eyes seemed to bore into Charlton. 'See folk come and go.'

'Uh-huh,' Linus said carefully as Cole paused.

'Day before yesterday I saw a feller come out of your bank. Not by the street door, though he went in that way. He left by the side door that opens directly from your office.'

36

Linus looked pale now, his face taut. The smile he forced didn't work, but he didn't speak.

'Big feller with a beard, wide shoulders, cannonball head, dressed well enough but wearing his gun low and tied down. That's what got my interest, so I looked a little more closely. Know the man I'm talking about?'

Linus shook his head, ran a tongue around his lips. He seemed to have forgotten the burning cigar and a long, sagging cylinder of ash dropped down the front of his waistcoat, but he didn't notice.

'He wouldn't've come out of my office. There's a short, narrow passage leads down from our file storage. It connects with the foyer one end, and behind a partition, to that side door at the other.'

'Doesn't sound like a good arrangement for keeping your bank secure, not if anyone can use it. But how would the feller I'm talking about know about it? This is the first time *I've* heard of it.'

Linus shrugged. 'It's no real secret, but it's hidden mostly by a couple of large potted plants. He may've just been poking around and noticed it. What're you getting at, anyway, Cole?' He tried to harden his voice but he was not successful.

'I know that man, Linus. He comes from Banjo Springs. He's called 'Quick' Quinlan. Dunno whether it refers to his claim to be half-brother to a bolt of lightning with a gun, or how ready he is to use his fists and boots. He enjoys crippling people.' He watched the tension taking hold of the banker, lowered his gaze to the bandaged hand, adding, 'He's Brack Devlin's troubleshooter.'

'Devlin? The man who runs the big gambling hall down in the Springs. Calls it a "casino"?'

'You know who I mean. Devlin's tough. They say he's got connections to a gambling syndicate on the East Coast.'

'I've heard that, too, but . . . I still don't know what you're getting at.'

'Linus, if you're in any kinda trouble, and Quinlan's part of it, you better tell me about it now.'

Charlton snorted, smiling crookedly. 'Trouble? Me? With people like that? What would I be doing dealing with Brack Devlin or—'

'Only way you'll deal with Devlin is through Quinlan – and I saw him leaving your office two days ago. And now you show up with busted fingers. One of Quinlan's little "demonstrations"? A kind of preview of what could happen?'

'I just told you, that door can be reached by—' The banker sounded annoyed and Cole broke in rudely.

'Know what you *told* me, Linus. Maybe it's so, maybe not. But Quinlan wouldn't traipse all the way up here to do business with your bank when Devlin already has his own set-up in Banjo Springs. If he came to see you, it was on behalf of Devlin.'

'Look, you're way off, Cole! I don't know what you're implying, exactly, but I have no dealings with this Quinlan, and certainly not with Brack Devlin! It would be more than my job's worth to get involved with a crook, and a *gambler* at that!'

Cole levelled his gaze at the banker and Linus could-n't hold the stare, dropped his eyes, involuntarily rubbing his bandaged hand lightly. He straightened his shoulders. 'I have to be going, Cole. I'll be obliged if you'll keep an eye on young Donny on the Fourth and—'

'Already said I would. Linus, before you go . . . I consider you a friend and if you have any problems, I'll be glad to help out.' He lifted a hand as the banker started to protest. 'I know Quinlan, and I've seen his work. I spent six months working for Careful Carmody on his freight line. Won't go into details but we made a run to Banjo and through no fault of his own, Carmody ran into trouble with Devlin. Devlin turned Quinlan loose. Carmody's retired now, still uses crutches. Me and the other freighters didn't fare too well, neither. I can give you the full story if you like, but take it from me, Linus, don't tangle with Quinlan. Bring me into it and I'll help you all I can.'

The banker began to bluster, working at it.

'I've had enough of this! Who d'you think you are, accusing me of dealing with the likes of Brack Devlin? I've tried to tell you—'

'Linus! Quinlan's the one to look out for. OK, he comes to see you, has a chat, mebbe over a cigar and whiskey, fairly pleasant . . .' He glanced pointedly at the injured hand. 'Fairly. But you've been warned now, just a hint of what might come your way. Wait, damnit! Let me finish. Next time won't be anywhere near so pleasant – there'll be a lot more than finger bones being cracked.'

Charlton was breathing hard now, his face deeply flushed, nostrils flaring, thick chest heaving. There was a lot of fear there but he was trying to cover it with anger.

'Damn you, Cole! Mind your own business! Now, that's all I have to say. Good-day!'

Cole watched him stride away angrily along the veranda, felt sudden aching pain in his hip and sat down again, using both hands to lift his leg back onto the rest.

He hoped he was wrong about Linus, but he knew he wasn't; the banker had somehow run foul of Devlin and his fixer had Linus in his sights.

He had been seriously thinking of moving on after the Seventh, but now . . . He'd already said it: he considerd the banker a friend and a man doesn't walk away from a friend in trouble.

The Fourth of July started with a bang – literally. Some farm boys, in for the celebrations, having to bring their wives to town early so they could help cook the goodies for breakfast and other meals, also brought in a good supply of moonshine. And gunpowder, in newspaper-wrapped packages in floursack carry bags slung across their chests and shoulders.

It was traditional that the law turned a blind eye to illicit stills at this time of year. In any case, sampling their neighbours' efforts meant passing several different stone jugs of the elixir from hand to hand. By the time a man had sipped all of the various brews, his taste-buds were numbed – and so was much of his brain.

No one was certain afterwards who first suggested they unlimber the Civil War cannon outside the council hall. The idea was to load it and salute The Flag, flapping desultorily at the top of the white-painted mast on the small lawn, with pyramids of cannonballs each side of the gun.

The moonshine was taking effect by the time a merry group ran the cannon out of its footings and into the small town square, deserted at this time; most of the activities were out at the barbecue pits and the fires of the designated cooking area, or in setting up tables at the old swimming hole.

Stumbling, staggering into one another, each man insisted on pouring some of his very own 'special' mix of gunpowder into the barrel. Their minds were too fuddled to keep count, and just in case there *had* been a short-count, they tossed in a few extra measures.Then they lit the fuse from a burning cigar and ran for cover.

Just as well they did.

The cannon exploded, hurling the breech and a portion of the barrel down a side street and clear over the roof of the double-storeyed Delta saloon. Pieces of shattered iron peppered and clattered against stores and houses; glass tinkled, wood splintered, frightened horses at hitch racks in connecting streets shied and whinnied, dogs ran whining for cover, cats raced, meowing in terror, up tall trees.

Irate citizens swarmed into the smoke-choked square – in Cole's case, *limped* in – but no one was to be seen. Only the shattered cannon and the broken gun-carriage. The flag pole was leaning at a new and potentially dangerous angle, too.

A slurring voice, its owner well hidden somewhere

41

not too far away, bawled, '*Hap-pee Independence Day!*'

And a half-dozen voices cut loose with Rebel yells.

That insane, booming blast set the tone for the rest of the day. It would be the noisiest, drunkenest celebration Barberry had ever seen.

There were several fights even before breakfast, but Cole, limping, his leg hurting like hell, let them sort themselves out. Mostly the combatants were too drunk to stand, let alone land damaging punches.

It was noisy, as was to be expected; fireworks were exploding and hissing and arcing all over the large picnic ground near the bend of the river. Smoke drifted in choking clouds, stung eyes, rasped nostrils. But no one seemed to mind. Everyone was here to have a good time – Hell, it was *Independence Day* – only happened once a year didn't it? And a damn good day to celebrate to the full. . . .

Cole knew he had to be lenient, turn a blind eye and not harry folk. Food seemed endless, the long wooden trestle-tables sagged under the weight of a hundred different dishes, prepared by the ladies of Barberry. The fiddlers started fiddling and flutes began trilling their sweet notes – not always playing the same tune. Someone produced an empty coal-oil drum, stole a couple of big ladles from the cooking area and wrapped the bowls in dishcloths. In minutes they had a booming bass drum, also throbbing to its own rhythm, the drummer bleary-eyed, lost in a fuzzy world of his own.But eventually, the musicians – or those posing as such – were prevailed upon to play the same tunes. The centre of the wooden platform was cleared and as the toe-tapping notes of *Turkey in the Straw* and *Buffalo Gals* filled the reeking air, the space became crowded with dancers.

There were many stumbles and elaborate, drink-slurred apologies. But when the men realized they were failing to impress their partners, insults were hurled, offence taken swiftly, followed by flying fists.

Most men were already way too drunk to cause injury, but Cole had to move in when a knife was drawn. Limping and gritting his teeth against his pain, he cracked two heads together and dragged the semi-conscious men away to sleep it off under some trees.

Trouble was, every time he went to someone's aid, there was always someone standing by to offer him a drink in appreciation of his efforts.

After a while, refusal not only became boring, but downright dangerous.

'Hey! This ain't panther piss, y' know! I been sweatin' over a hot still for nigh on two weeks, so don't you insult me by refusin' my liquor, Sher'f!'

He escaped a couple of wildly swinging bottles but had consumed a good deal of liquor himself after realizing the raw brew deadened the knifing pain of his wound. Would it do the same for the other pain on the Seventh? He underestimated the powerful effects of the moonshine. It caught up with him suddenly, unexpectedly. Waves of dizziness and queasiness overwhelmed him and he ran staggeringly for the shadows of some trees to rest up a spell. Just a minute or two. *Wait. Where was Donny Charlton?* He hadn't seen the boy for a while;

last time was down at the swimming hole with a bunch of his friends. He had sent Josh and Joel Miller down that way to keep an occasional eye on the boy. He had better go and check with them and. . . .

Sudden illness ambushed him and Donny Charlton slipped from his mind.

Wiping his mouth, he only now realized that it was quite dark under the trees here, heading towards sundown. Where the hell had the day gone? He leaned against a tree, head swimming. Maybe he'd sit and have a smoke, then go look for the kid and. . . .

The fist came out of nowhere, drove into his kidney area and slammed him face first into the rough bark of the tree. Lights burst and whirled behind his eyes; he had enough sense to know they weren't Fourth of July firecrackers. Then his legs were kicked out from under him. A boot thudded into his upper chest. A worn heel drove down towards his face. He managed to wrench his head aside just in time, but the heel tore part of his ear. The searing pain sent some sort of sanity through his throbbing brain.

He twisted the foot next time it came swinging in and heaved mightily. Someone yelled, and there were stumbling sounds and curses.

'Kick his goddamn leg wound! *Hurt* the son of a bitch, Quick said. *Do* it!'

That sure didn't sound like just a couple of over-exuberant townsmen! These men were out to hurt him – and badly. He rolled, head spinning, still nauseous, somehow got the tree between himself and his attackers. In the shadows and with his sight blurred from the drink and that initial blow to his kidneys, he could only make out the men as hazy, moving shapes. He twisted violently as a boot drove towards his wounded upper thigh. It missed, but his leg crumpled under him and he fell to one knee. He used his hands to slap away a kick aimed at his face. He up-ended the boot's owner and staggered to his feet, pressing his back into the tree for support. His throbbing leg threatened to collapse again. The second man swung hard. Cole ducked and the man howled as his fist hit the tree full force. While he sucked his popped and cut knuckles, Cole hooked him in the belly, spread a hand over the dimly outlined face and smashed his head against the tree. The attacker started to crumple, moaning.

The other man had regained his balance and came in with a roar, swinging. All the while firecrackers exploded, rockets soared, strident music as well as Rebel yells all drowned out the sounds of the fight.

Cole's leg wouldn't support him any longer. He put out a hand as he started to fall and a knee drove into his face, flinging him back. He struck the tree and sprawled, clawing at the ground, trying to push upright.

But they were onto him now, fists and boots flailing, maiming, grunted words punctuated by the effort behind each blow.

'Mind your – own – goddamn – business in – future!'

'An' – here's somethin' – to help you – re – remember!'

There was an abrupt explosion of light. Then he was tumbling into pitch blackness, racked and jarred with thudding pain. . . .

His ears were ringing, his head exploding, filled with noise as if he was standing inside a ringing church bell. And, dimly, through the racket and disorientation, he heard a distant voice:

'Here he is! Behind this tree. Oh, Jesus, he's been in a fight. Aaagh! Smell him!'

'Drunk as a skunk! He's been hittin' the moonshine!'

'Throw some water over him!'

Even through his pain and all the racket, Cole recognized that voice. 'Li – Linus?'

'Yes, damn you, it's me! Where the hell've you been? We've been looking for you for over an hour . . .' He was shaken roughly. 'Goddamnit, Cole! Don't you pass out on me again! While you've been getting drunk and fighting, young Donny's gone missing! You were s'posed to be watching out for him. *Damnit! Wake up!* D'you hear me? I said *Donny's – gone!*'

CHAPTER 5

LOST BOY

Cole was ashamed. He could rationalize a lot of things: pain in the leg wound, rotgut literally forced upon him or there would be hostility and so more trouble to watch out for, and a quiet eagerness on his own part to use the moonshine to deaden other pains that waited just below the horizon, a couple of days away. He could use all these things to tell himself it wasn't his fault: the booze was way too strong, the pain in his leg was intense because he had refused to use a stick at the celebration. But it all came down to one fact: *he got drunk and he was derelict in his duty.*

Donny Charlton was missing and no one knew for just how long. Someone looked around for him late in the afternoon and he just wasn't there, nor anywhere to be found.

All the men, including a distraught and very angry Linus Charlton, were searching the brush and the swimming hole; Donny was a good swimmer, but there were dead trees and other potential snags awaiting the unwary beneath the surface.

Bess was being comforted by the other women and the Independence Day celebrations had now come to an abrupt halt. No fireworks criss-crossed the night sky, no fiddles or Jews' harps filled the balmy air with blood-pounding tunes and much of the uneaten food was spoiled. The coffee pots were continually refilled, though, as weary, unsuccessful searchers staggered in looking for something warm and stimulating.

Cole himself had dunked his head in the swimming hole several times, wanting to change his smelly clothes, but reluctant to leave the scene. He was already the target of many hostile and silently accusing stares.

The Miller boys, Josh and Joel, had done their duty well enough; they had checked on Donny's where-abouts frequently, and there had been nothing unto-ward. Once his playmate, young Sam Bale, got into trouble in the swimming hole and Donny had helped him ashore. Sam had actually fallen in, his clothes got wet and he became cold. Donny, in a rare gesture of generosity, gave him his jacket to keep him warm.

'Donny wasn't makin' no trouble,' Josh Miller told Cole and the tight-lipped banker. 'Playin' with his friends. Aw, they got a bit cheeky a few times, played pranks, but someone usually stopped things before they got outta hand.'

He looked at his brother for confirmation and Joel nodded. 'They was mostly swimmin', it bein' such a hot day.' He broke off and his gaze was shifty as he glanced at Linus and looked away hurriedly. 'I reckon – sorry,

Banker, but seems logical to me – that if we can't find Donny anywheres around the picnic grounds then. . . .' He jerked his head towards the river.

'No!' snapped Charlton, his well-fed lower jaw trembling. 'No, Donny was a good swimmer! He hasn't drowned!'

'Maybe we better drag the hole, Linus,' Cole said quietly. 'Seems Joel might have something.'

Linus glared at the contrite sheriff. 'I doubt that anyone here will take much notice of your opinions after today, *Sheriff*! I suggest you go home and change those filthy clothes and sleep it off! You aren't much use to anyone right now.'

That hurt Cole but he tried to keep a straight face. 'I can stand my stink a little longer.' He turned to the Millers. 'You boys go organize a dragline. . . .'

Charlton grabbed Cole's shoulder and spun him hard enough to make him stagger; pain shot through his leg and he slapped the banker's hand away. It must have hurt because Linus winced and snatched his arm back to his chest, nursing it with his bandaged left hand.

'I'm still sheriff, Linus. Maybe I won't be tomorrow, but for tonight I'm still wearing the badge and I don't have time to waste on stupid arguments. I know I've behaved badly but that won't help us find Donny. Now, you Millers go do what I told you.'

The brothers hurried away and Charlton gave Cole a hard look, mouth tight.

'I'll never forgive you if anything's . . . happened to that boy, Cole!'

The sheriff met his gaze. 'If something has, I'll never forgive myself, Linus.'

It was a terrible night. Bonfires were lit and the search continued, even though no one considered it ideal conditions for looking.

The men were tired, their weariness increased by the earlier heavy drinking and gluttony. No one really thought they would do a thorough job and an hour or so after midnight, Cole called a halt. He had done as much searching as the others but knew it was hopeless in the dark.

'No, damnit!' gasped the puffing, sweating, staggering banker. 'We are not abandoning this search!'

'Show some sense, Linus,' Cole said wearily. 'Look at these men. Look at yourself. This isn't a search party, it's a bunch of stumblebums. The men are half-asleep, and with hangovers working on them. You can't expect good results – *any* worthwhile results. I think we've pretty well established Donny's not lying on the bottom of the swimming hole, but if he's hurt somewhere, in this brush, and all the shadows, we could walk past him without even knowing he's there.

'If – if he is hurt,' Linus huffed, 'it's important we find him and – get him medical help as soon as possible.'

They all agreed but backed Cole: no search was going to be successful in the dark. Some of the men were being dragged away by their womenfolk now, others just wandered off, stupid with fatigue.

Linus dropped onto a tree-stump, shoulders

slumped, looking down at the ground between his feet.

'I'll give you a hand home, Linus.'

The banker looked up at Cole. 'Go rest your leg! I hope you wake with the god-*damndest* hangover!' He rose, swaying. 'Where – where's Bess?'

'Some of the women took her home earlier. . . .'

'How am I going to face her?'

'It was my fault. D'you want me to come in and—'

'I want nothing from you, Cole! Nothing. Except to find that boy, unharmed! Now get your hands off my arm.'

Linus shook the sheriff off and lurched away, mopping his grimy face.

Cole, silent, grim, limped back towards the Star hotel.

The next long, long day's search was fruitless, a shambles.

Hangovers killed any real efforts the sick and sorry men tried to make. But they did establish that there were no real tracks; there had been too many kids running about all over the picnic area and particularly around the swimming hole. Cole's questioning, done with squinted eyes and shaking hands so he could barely read the notes he took, produced nothing worthwhile.

Sure, everyone had seen Donny – or at least had seen half a dozen tow-headed boys frolicking and getting up to mischief – and no one had taken any particular notice. There were several strangers in town, but none of them seemed particularly interested in the boys'

51

activities. Most, like the locals, had been looking for free booze and grub.

One man was mentioned, wearing a dark-green shirt, and Cole propped up his ears at that. Some dark-green cloth, obviously torn from a shirt, had been found near where he had fought the men who had jumped him.

The description of the man was vague: average height and build, looked like a cowboy, hard-drinking.

No one could put a name to him.

Later in the day Bess arrived with a few other women, bringing lunch for the searchers. She looked terrible. Normally a handsome woman, she was pale and drawn and her nostrils seemed pinched in, her mouth pursed, giving her a forlorn yet angry look.

She walked right up to Cole, who was leaning on his stick, trying to ignore the ache in his leg, and slapped him once across the face. It turned his head on his shoulders and silence fell around him. He blinked back tears stinging his eyes, looked down at her as her bosom heaved with tremendous emotion.

All he did was nod slowly, admitting he deserved the slap. She turned and lunged away, her hands covering her face, her shoulders shaking with sobs.

Somehow he got through the day but he was still suffering the after-effects of the moonshine when darkness fell and the search was abandoned until tomorrow.

He went to bed without food.

There was grey, cheerless light filling his hotel room when Cole slowly swam up through waves of sleep, wincing at the racket of a fist hammering at his door.

'Jesus Christ!' he said, holding his throbbing head. The thunder at the door kept on. 'Who the hell is it? What's up?'

'It's Linus. Open this door at once!'

Cole winced. He couldn't even see clearly. He groped for clothes and sat on the edge of the bed, barely able to move. *That damn rotgut! It was still affecting him!*

What in the hell did they put in that moonshine! His head was exploding, his belly felt as if it had been ripped out, aflame, as if he had swallowed acid. He moaned as he bent forward an inch at a time, trying to find his trouser legs with his feet.

The pounding started on the door again.

'Linus, I swear I'll gutshoot you, you don't get away from that goddamn door!'

He clutched his head again at the sound of his own raised voice. *God, he was so damn tired. . . .*

'Can you hurry it up, Cole? This is important.' The banker sounded more reasonable this time, his voice had a tremor in it. 'Very – important.'

'Linus, if I thought you'd done this a'purpose, battered on my door at this ungodly hour just to roust me for . . . whatever the hell it is I did or didn't do. Mind's like a swamp. Can't think clear.'

'It's – it's about Donny!' Charlton's voice was quieter now, the tremor more noticeable.

Cole frowned, squinting, his eyes almost closed. *Donny.* Any news sounded like it was going to be bad.

'Be but a coupla minutes, Linus,' he called, reeling again from the sound of his own raised voice.

53

Wearing only trousers, he padded to the door, unlocked it. There were still wall lamps burning in the hotel passage and he held one arm across his eyes as the banker hurried in. The hangover seemed worse today, increased by fatigue.

Cole closed the door and leaned against it, favouring the left leg, bending it slightly and taking most of his weight on the good leg. He squinted at the banker, blinked, trying to clear his vision.

The man looked positively appalling. He was still wearing the clothes Cole had last seen him in at the river. His stubble was showing, and, with the shadows flickering in the room as Cole lit a match and applied it to the table lamp wick, Linus's face was gaunt, despite its normal chubby look. His eyes were sunken and his mouth seemed to pull back tightly against his teeth.

'You look like hell. What's happened?'

Linus Charlton sank down onto the edge of the bed, the bandage on his left hand now grubby and grey, a part of it frayed and dangling. He raised his haunted eyes and his face tightened a little as he looked at the sheriff, who was obviously not in the best of shape himself.

'I – I've called off the search.'

Cole stiffened, felt his belly swirl. 'Ah, no, Linus! Not that! He – he's surely – all right. . . ?'

'How do I know? How the devil do I know anything about him? Whether he's all right, hurt, been knocked about or—'

'Whoa, man! What the hell're you saying? What're you talking about?'

Charlton continued to stare for long moments and Cole thought he had passed into some sort of a trance. Then he stirred and began feeling in the pockets of his dirty, torn coat. He produced a crumpled piece of paper, smoothed it out on one of his fat thighs and stared at it for another long, silent spell. Then, without looking up, he lifted the hand with the paper in it, offering it to Cole.

The sheriff took the paper, moved closer to the lamp. His vision was slowly improving but he had to squint and turn the paper this way and that to read the words crudely printed upon it in pencil:

The kid's OK. He'll stay that way long as you get $20,000 dollars together and keep it handy.

We'll tell you when and how to pay it over. We're not joking banker. Do what we say and you can have the kid back.

Cole read it again, looked up at the banker, sitting on the edge of the bed, shoulders sagging. He wouldn't have been surprised to see a tear running down the grimy, stubbled cheeks.

'Where did this come from, Linus?'

'Pushed under the bank door. I – I went back to change. I keep some spare clothes in my office and didn't want to go home and disturb Bess. She'd taken so long to go to sleep and . . .' He paused, sighing, shaking his head. 'I was stunned, sat there at my desk, just – staring at it, reading the words over and over, as if they would tell me something. . . .'

'You know what it is, of course?'

Charlton nodded slowly, but his voice was hoarse when he answered: 'Of course I know what it is! It's a – a ransom note. They – someone has kidnapped Donny and wants me to pay twenty-thousand dollars to get him back!' He scrubbed a hand down his face. 'Where the hell am I going to get that kind of money?'

Cole frowned. 'Linus, you're president of the local bank—'

The banker's head snapped up. 'Do you think I could touch the bank money! Don't be a damn fool!'

'Surely they'd bend the rules, lend you the money to pay the ransom? You've served them well for years. . . .'

'You don't understand these people, Cole. They have stockholders from overseas, England, Scotland, Europe. Those men're thousands of miles away. They're not interested in some Wild West kidnapping! They want *dividends*, not debts!'

Cole scratched his aching head. 'I believe they'd help you out, Linus, but if not . . . there's Bess, isn't there? It's her child and she has a good deal of money if I'm to believe the talk.'

The banker scoffed. 'Talk! Yes, there's been lots of talk – and it's mostly true. Curtis, her first husband, left her pretty well-off. But it's all tied up in property and investments. There is a trust fund for the boy's education and so on and that can't be touched by anyone except his uncle, Carl, who's executor of his brother's will. Bess has access to a small amount for 'expenses' and while it's quite liberal, it's nowhere near the ransom these . . . bastards demand.'

'This Carl . . . can't he be approached? Donny's his nephew. Surely he'll release funds for the ransom?'

'As well he might! But he's a lawyer, Cole – dots every 'i', crosses every 't'. Knows all the legal books backwards. Even if he saw fit to somehow bend his rules, how long d'you think it'd take? With him in San Francisco!'

Cole's leg was throbbing and he sat down on the bed beside the banker.

'I don't see what else you can do, Linus. Approach the bank or this Carl Curtis. If it was me, I'd certainly appeal to the bank.'

'I'd rather they didn't know anything about it.' Linus looked uncomfortable under Cole's quizzical stare. 'I mean – well, you wouldn't understand. When you're responsible for so much money, every day, and there's even a hint of – problems, that could *involve* money . . .' He shrugged. 'Even though I'm on good terms with head office – well, I don't know, Cole.'

'Then you have to go to Carl, through Bess.'

'I – don't want to bother her with this. She's so – so distraught—'

'Goddamit, Linus! Pull yourself together! You need to raise that money, you have two chances to do it – and you don't want to try either one! You've got to make a decision, man! And be damn quick about it.'

Charlton didn't seem to have heard. He was holding the note again, lips moving slightly as he read.

'If I can't raise the money, they – they'll kill him.'

'I doubt it. They do that and there'll be no chance of them getting their hands on twenty-thousand dollars.'

It was pathetic to see the ray of hope flash across Linus's ravaged face. Cole looked away.

They might not kill Donny – but they could well begin mutilating him, send back an ear, or some fingers. . . .

'What a helluva lousy deal,' he said aloud.

CHAPTER 6

TURNING POINT

Bess was appalled at the news.

Linus was nervous and mumbled a lot and having to ask him to repeat everything made Bess really mad, jarred her out of her comfortless lethargy. Grief turned to anger.

'Kidnapped! My God, Linus! You've truly excelled yourself this time!'

'Are you mad, woman? It's not my fault! I specifically asked that damn sheriff to keep a special eye on Donny. If you're looking for someone to blame, blame Adam Cole!'

'Oh, I will – I do. But don't think it lets you off the hook!'

She started one of her tirades and Linus snapped, grabbed her by the shoulders – hurting his broken fingers but uncaring – and shook her until her head rocked violently on her shoulders. The words stopped and she looked startled, groped at him for support. He thrust her roughly from him and she stumbled back. She sat down heavily in an overstuffed armchair. She stared up at him apprehensively.

'You silly woman! This is no time to be looking for someone to blame! We have to get the ransom organized. You have to get Carl to send the money by telegraphic transfer or an authority for us to draw against the trust. I can arrange the bank's end of it but he'll have to expedite things. I haven't had a time limit named by the kidnappers but I'm sure it will be only a matter of days.'

His words got through and she realized the truth of what he said. 'Surely it will be faster for you to make some arrangement through the bank? Borrow the ransom?'

His face tightened and he shook his head. 'No. No, I don't want to ask this of head office. You've no idea the complicated procedure. An intensive investigation of us both – even an audit of our accounts. In fact they might choose to do a complete audit of the bank at the same time. I can't handle that and this crisis as well.'

'For heaven's sake, Linus! Tell them how urgent it is!'

Again he shook his head, his mouth a tight line. 'It will cut no ice, Bess, believe me. I know the system. It'll be much faster and satisfactory to have Carl wire us authority and put up the money. After all, it's for his nephew.'

Her damp eyes narrowed and she frowned. 'Is there something you haven't told me, Linus? Have you had . . . trouble with head office, over your books or some other. . . ?'

'Goddamnit, *no*! It's nothing like that. I just know what I'm dealing with here and it comes right down to this, Bess. If we want to see Donny alive again, we have to pay the ransom! Now, be sensible, get changed and I'll walk you down to the telegraph office so you can get some wires away to California.'

She sat there, hands clasped in her lap, fingers tearing at the delicate lace of a perfumed kerchief, looking up at him without a trace of affection.

'Of course I'll do this, Linus. But I still think it would be quicker for you to arrange it through the bank.'

'For God's sake, woman! *Will* you get changed!'

Breathing heavily, he started for the door.

'Your concern for Donny is admirable, Linus,' she said with heavy sarcasm. 'Considering how you feel about him.'

He paused, hand on the doorknob. 'He's only a boy, Bess. Give me some credit for genuine concern.'

'Well, I suppose there's a lot of guilt behind it. If not, there ought to be!'

He managed not to slam the door behind him.

It was the seventh of July.

Cole rode out of town early, headed for a place where he could overlook the river and the field where the Fourth's celebrations had taken place. There was a little activity there, a few men scouting around, looking for sign that might come in handy later.

He ought to be down there with them, he supposed, but – no. This was a special day to him and he preferred to be alone. Rolling a cigarette while sitting on a rock, his wounded leg straight out, boot resting a few inches above the ground between two rocks, he glanced at his grazing mount, a dappled grey mare. There was a bottle of bar whiskey in the saddlebags. It might be marginally better than the moonshine that had affected him so badly on Independence Day. Usually, he drank a full bottle, sometimes more, on July 7 – he had for the past five years, anyway.

But – maybe not today. Maybe it was time to just sit and think and remember *why*. . . .

He had been alone since he was a button. Dragged around the cattle trails by his widowed father from the age of four, virtually reared by trail cooks and rough cowboys.

His father was killed trying to stop a stampede when the boy was six and he was passed from hand to hand amongst the trail men. Fortunately, he was intelligent and learned something of the rugged, dangerous life. He could rope and brand and ride, repair wagons, skin-out a slaughtered cow or a deer – many times the deer had been hunted, stalked and shot by him.

Ailing horses and cows frightened him at first but soon he learned how to treat their problems, or, if they weren't treatable, to put them out of their misery as painlessly as possible.

There were men who enjoyed watching animals suffer, he found. And there were men who made these sadistic types suffer, too. So, by watching, and later by experience, he learned how to use his fists – and later still, how to use his guns.

He was a natural good rifle shot. Once a well-known gunfighter rode with the herd for a few days – obviously on the run from the law – and when two representatives of that law caught up with him, Cole saw how the man had earned his reputation. He wounded both deputies and the trail boss, pretty damn courageously, after witnessing the speed of the gunfight, ran the *pistolero* off with a shotgun. He cared for the wounded lawmen, took a detour to a town so they could get proper medical attention.

'Weren't you scared, boss?' Cole had asked. 'I mean, you seen how fast he was with a gun and he was sure ready to use it. . . .'

'Don't admire him, kid,' the trail boss told him curtly. 'Bein' fast with a gun is nothin' much. You think such a man is popular. He ain't. A lot of the time, it's just that folk are plain scared of him, don't want to rub him up the wrong way. So they pretend to admire him. Oh, some actually do, of course, but all in all, bein' a gunfighter ain't anythin' to be proud of. Pride's for the man who earns the respect of his pards.'

Later, one of the wranglers told him that the boss had once been a gunfighter, but one of his bullets wounded a child and he hadn't worn a six-gun since; swore he never would.

A nighthawk was killed in an Indian raid one night and the trail boss handed the man's Colt rig to the boy – now approaching his teens.

'This is a good weapon, son. You need to carry one if you aim to follow the cattle trails.' The trail boss paused. 'You dunno nothin' about handguns, do you? You're OK with a rifle, but a Colt, no. Well, I'll teach you how to take 'em apart and put 'em back together blindfolded.'

'Why would I want to do it blindfolded?'

' 'Cause sometime you might be in a bind in the dark and you'll need to be able to recognize each part of your gun and its workin's by touch. Might never happen, but if it does . . . you get to see the sunrise.'

The trail boss, calling himself simply 'Montana' now, kept his word and Cole turned out to be a good pupil.

'Will you show me a fast draw?'

'Son, I will not. I'll show you a *safe* draw, so you don't shoot your own foot off or your hoss, or even your saddle mate if he's close by. But you won't need a lightnin'-quick draw.'

'How d'you know? S'pose I find I do need a slick draw – and can't do it. I'm dead.'

The trail boss, a grizzled man pushing sixty, worked his jaws on his chaw of tobacco and spat a stream, never taking his rheumy grey eyes off the youngster.

'Thing is, son, you can show a man all the short cuts you know – but it's up to him to use them as fast as he's able – and some men just ain't able. *That*'s what gets 'em killed: believin' they know how to make a slick draw – and when it comes down to doin' it the only fast thing they get is a funeral.'

But twice he caught the kid behind the chuck wagon, testing himself, whipping out his Colt from the dead nighthawk's rig. He was pretty good, but fumbled a lot.

At last the boss took him aside.

'You disappoint me, boy. Why you so damn keen to learn how to draw fast?'

' 'Cause my father never could draw fast and it near got him killed when I was just a shaver. I was never so scared in my life, wonderin' if he'd die or recover.'

The trail boss frowned. 'Who looked after you while he was recoverin'?'

The kid looked at him steadily. 'I looked after myself. An' him, too. The man who shot him left us out in the desert.'

'He left you too?' The boss was outraged. 'By God, what kinda snake was he, this fast gun?'

The kid's gaze didn't waver. 'A dead one – eventually. After I caught up with him.'

'How old were you?'

Cole shrugged. 'I dunno – eight, mebbe, coulda been nine or ten. . . .'

The trail boss didn't ask any more, but he took the Colt from the kid and showed him how his grip was wrong, how the holster was too low, and how cutting out a piece of leather to allow the finger to reach the trigger at the moment of draw was a definite advantage.

Once again, the kid was an apt pupil.

'I ever hear of you tryin' to make a name for yourself as a fast gun, I'll come after you. There's a trick or two I ain't taught you and it'll gimme the edge if I have to chase you down.'

Cole never went looking for trouble. Once or twice he had to put his acquired gun-speed to use. Mostly, if he used the Colt at all it was during a trail drive – or when doing ranch work. For he drifted around, took a variety of jobs, all connected with cattle. It was all he knew and he enjoyed the life, meeting the tough rannies who rode these trails, living out lonely winters in line shacks, talking to the cows and the wild animals on occasion, just to hear his own voice.

He knew women in the trail towns, he 'saw the elephant', but he often stared longingly at ranchers in from their spreads, with wives and families. He didn't recall his mother very well but he knew she had been soft and kind and had made him feel good.

But a wife and ranch was out of reach of a drifting trail hand who could barely write, like him. He knew that.The rough cowboys joshed him when they saw him in one of his dreamy moods.

'Cole, you ever see a rich cowboy? I mean for more'n a few days? If he's got money, he spends it, recovers from a bender and lousy hangover, then what does he do? Go trailin' again, works his butt off, and does the same blame thing all over ... *That*'s a cowboy's life. There ain't many married ones. I mean, what woman'd want a man who wasn't gonna sit across the supper table from her more'n a coupla times a year?'

So he started saving his money. Sure, he painted a few towns red with his pards, but he had an arrangement with a small bank in Denver where he could deposit money by telegraph. At trail's end, on pay-day, his first stop was at a telegraph station where he laboriously filled out the necessary forms and got his bank account number from the greasy slip of paper a clerk had written it on for him and sent off a few dollars.

Those of the crew who knew, joshed him, often asked him for a loan, but knew it would never be forthcoming.

They made fun of him but he had the last laugh: he met Alice Brown in a town where the herd was flood-bound for two weeks.

At the end of that time, he quit the trail herd and the boss was generous enough to pay him the bonus he would've earned if he had completed the drive.

He and Alice were married and he took up a quarter-section and homesteaded it. They had a boy child, named him Jeff, after Alice's dead father, and Cole knew he had found what he had been searching for all those years without even realizing it: happiness and comfort in the form of a beautiful, loving woman, a healthy son and a small ranch that would soon expand. *Satisfaction*, that's what it was; at long last he had found himself a satisfactory life.

Then three days after the community had celebrated one Independence Day, some kids playing with left-over fireworks shot a rocket into a loaded haywagon parked against the west wall of the log house.

Cole was out on the range, fencing, when he first saw the smoke. He hit the saddle at a dead run and rode straight as an arrow towards the flames he could now see shooting up above the hogback rise.

It was too late. A warped door he had been meaning to fix had jammed and Alice and the boy had been overcome by smoke. Although the neighbours had the fire out quickly, it wasn't quick enough to save his family.

The boy would have been six years old now, his birthday being the Seventh of July.

Instead of celebrating the boy's progress through life, for the past five years Adam Cole had drunk himself senseless each July 7, drowning thoughts of what might have been. . . .

But not this time!

This time he could do something about *saving* a boy and he would need to be as sober as a bishop.

In a moment of new resolve he took the whiskey bottle and smashed it against the rocks. He watched the dark-brown liquid trickle away, soak into the earth.

Whether he were successful in finding Donny Charlton, or not, he realized he had reached some kind of turning point this day.

The tragedies and happiness of the past were still there. Nothing had changed, never could change.

But he could.

And this was the time.

CHAPTER 7

THE STRANGERS

It was after sundown on July 8 when Cole rode slowly back into town, the weary grey plodding towards the livery. The hostler helped him down from the saddle and the sheriff, grimy from long trails, leaned against the stall post and massaged his aching leg.

'How's the wound comin', Cole?'

'I can tell you it's still there,' the sheriff growled, then smiled crookedly, softening his tone. 'It's not too bad, Earl. If those hardcases hadn't massaged it with their boots I'd be running like a deer now.'

The hostler nodded soberly, took his pipe from his leathery lips, sniffed deeply through his bulbous nose. 'They was strangers, but I think I've seen the one in the green shirt before. Rode in with that Quinlan feller few days earlier but stayed on for the Fourth.'

That news earned the livery man a sharp look. 'Why the hell didn't you tell me? I've covered half the damn county these past couple of days, trying to get a line on him and his pard. Reckon they're connected to the kidnapping.'

The hostler sniffed again, moved his feet uneasily. 'Well, I dunno who he is, Cole. Just recollected he came in with Quinlan.'

'Yeah, all right, Earl. Take care of the horse.'

As the sheriff took down his rifle and warbag, Earl said, 'Linus asked me to tell you, when you showed he wants to see you.' He paused, then added, 'Poor devil looks like death warmed over. 'Course, that Bess ain't makin' things any easier for him.'

Cole nodded and headed back to his room at the Star. He ordered hot water for a bath and afterwards shaved. Halfway through there was a knock on the door and Linus Charlton came hurrying in.

'I've had a second note,' he said, without preamble. He produced a crumpled piece of paper and offered it to Cole.

The sheriff saw it was the same printing as before:

Better hurry with that money
This is just to show we really
do have the kid.
Next time it could be a finger

Linus held up a tuft of greasy, tow-coloured hair. 'All Bess said was "They might've let him wash his hair!" ' He shook his head jerkily, his drawn, greyish face tightening. 'Damn woman.'

The banker looked terrible: he had dark smears under his eyes, his jowls were drooping, even his neck

70

seemed scrawny. He still wore a bandage on his left hand and it looked to be the same grimy one from a couple of days ago.

'Where've you been, Cole? Damnit, man, I need to have you close by for this thing.'

'Rode around to see everyone I could remember being at the celebration and who didn't come from town. Didn't learn much. Most folk saw Donny and some playmate, Sam Bale, but no one saw them leave the area. Didn't get as far out as the Bale place or the Bowden spread, but I'll take a packhorse later and cover more ground.'

'Well, I dunno how much more time they aim to give me to get the ransom. I'd be obliged if you'd stay close.'

'Linus, you do your part with the ransom. I'll do what I can from my side. Have you got the OK for the money yet?'

Charlton heaved a sigh. 'Yes – and no. I mean, Carl Curtis, after a slew of wires sent in Bess's name, finally agreed to allow access to the trust funds – but it's gotta be done through my bank's head office. The very thing I was trying to avoid!'

Cole frowned. 'Makes it easier, doesn't it?'

'You might think so.' There was a dull sound to Linus's words. 'Now, as well as all this worry, and making the arrangements, I have to write *reports* which amount to little more than 'Please Explain' – and that's ridiculous. What can you say about a kidnapping, other than it happened?' He rubbed hard at his head, shaking it. 'I haven't slept more than two hours straight since I last saw you.'

71

'Looks like it, too. Linus, you'd better take or, better still, *make* time so you have a break. Once they want the ransom, you'll be working like a berserk beaver and its just the time you'll need all your wits about you. If you don't get it right, for some reason. . . .'

Linus nodded. 'I know. Bess blames me – oh, you, too, equally, I think. She's relentless in her criticism. I – I even hoped at one stage that the kid would turn up – dead. Just to have the blasted thing finished with.'

'You wouldn't want that to happen,' Cole said slowly and Linus knew *he* meant he wouldn't want it to happen, either.

He didn't know about Cole's past and the loss of his own son five years earlier, but for some time he had suspected a tragedy somewhere along Cole's backtrail.

'When will you have the money ready?'

'If I can stall head office on these unnecessary "reports", tomorrow afternoon, maybe. I – I'm going to count it myself and package it. That way there'll be no mistakes, and it should keep those fools in Denver off my neck.'

'You ought to have someone with you to check, Linus. That's what will keep head office off you. And it'll be better if anyone claims there's been a mistake.'

'No! I *want* to do this myself as far as possible, Cole. I have to square myself with Bess and if I can take credit for getting the ransom paid and bringing Donny back safely. . . .'

Cole could see the man's reasoning: he was probably more afraid of Bess than of his superiors in Denver but he would never admit it.

72

'Cole, I need to ask you another favour.' The sheriff waited, face unreadable. 'Will – will you deliver the ransom? Oh, I know there're no arrangements yet, but – well, you're experienced in handling this kind of thing.'

'No, I'm not, Linus. I've never been involved in a kidnapping pay-off. But if they're agreeable to me handing over the ransom, I'll do it.'

He was surprised at the relief that showed on the banker's face. It seemed the man was close to collapse and now some of the tension drained away – visibly.

'I – I'm much obliged, Cole, very much obliged.'

Then Linus wheeled and fumbled at the door, and stumbled out into the passage, leaving the door swinging.

Cole slowly closed it, frowning.

Because payment instructions for the ransom seemed imminent, Sheriff Cole did not make his planned extended ride out to the edges of the county, interviewing people who had attended the Independence Day celebrations.

As Banker Charlton had pointed out, when instructions came they would likely have to be acted upon pronto. Linus was ready to go, now that the bank's head office had at last approved release of the money. In fact the Denver people sent extra funds down in a strongbox on a special stage run, to supplement what Linus's safe already held. $20,000 was one hell of a lot of money.

No wonder Denver was nervous.

Cole had escorted the strongbox from the depot to the bank and then Linus locked himself in his office, preparing the ransom, taking full responsibility.

Feeling edgy, with it being more or less general knowledge that part of the ransom had arrived and was being counted in the bank, Cole stayed in town, on the balcony outside his hotel room. Using field glasses he watched the bank and its surrounds, noting everyone who entered the building.

He was bored after a while but admitted the enforced rest was helping his leg's recovery. He barely limped at all now, though he couldn't run yet – jog-trot for a short distance, maybe, but no more.

He swept the glasses around town and some of the country that he could see beyond the outskirts. The lenses were good quality, Army issue, but still not good enough to pick out the features of riders approaching the town, entering by way of the short adobe bridge at the southern end of Front Street.

That was how he missed recognizing the two men who drifted in, several minutes apart. One was forking a big black, the other a dirty-white gelding. They both made for the livery and he moved the glasses back to the bridge trail, then slowly around the outskirts.

He jumped when shortly afterwards a piping voice behind him called his name. 'Sher'f Cole. . . ?'

He spun round, regretting it as pain shot through his leg. He stared at a freckle-faced boy in ragged patched overalls, only one strap holding the garment up.

'What d'you want, son?'

74

'I'm Toddy. My father runs the stables. He sent me to find you.'

'What's up, Toddy?'

'He said to tell you that the feller in the green shirt's just arrived – only he ain't wearin' a green shirt today. It's faded blue. And he was ridin' a black geldin'.'

Cole was tense. 'Where is he?'

'Turned his mount in for groomin'. Pa's doin' it—'

'Was he alone?'

The kid scratched his head – another towhead, Cole noticed. The town seemed full of them. 'Might've been someone with him – another feller arrived a coupla minutes after him. He had a grey shirt an' was wearin' a tatty old vest over it. I – I think they knew each other, but din' let on, you know?'

'You're pretty bright, Toddy, noticing something like that. You couldn't be mistaken?'

'No, sir. Not the way they looked at each other and the one in the blue shirt kind of – nodded, but hardly moved his head. Like this.'

Cole gave the boy a dime and, as the kid ran off down the length of the balcony, went into his room and picked up his rifle from where he had left it in a corner.

He locked the door behind him and hurried down the stairs into the hotel foyer.

Using the back alleys, he made his way to the law office, entered by the rear door and placed his rifle beside the battered desk; if the men he wanted to see saw him walking the streets with a rifle in hand, they might be scared off.

And he didn't want that: he wanted to know what

they were up to. Someone had to deliver those ransom notes.

It was approaching sundown and long shadows began to mottle the streets. Men who worked in town at the stores and the small sawmill, the stage depot and so on, closed up shop and many of them made their way to Mannering's Delta saloon to sink a few beers and maybe a whiskey, if they could afford it, before heading home to supper.

Cole felt like a drink, had done for a couple of days, but hadn't been game to give in. He was still afraid he might capitulate and throw his annual drunk – he sure had his head full of Alice and Jeff. It was normal for him at this time of year, but with the ransom payment looming, he couldn't afford any diversions.

Still, he entered the saloon, scanned the drinkers at the bar and the tables scattered around the smoky room. The men Toddy had warned him about, Blue Shirt and Vest, as he thought of them, were sitting at a table near a side door. He let his gaze slide across them without pause.

He greeted a few townsfolk, breasted the bar and ordered a beer, using the large mirror to watch the two men who claimed his interest. They, in turn, were surreptitiously watching him, but he merely leaned an elbow on the counter and rolled a cigarette, chatting with one of the sweating barkeeps. He lit up and shook out the vesta, eyes still a little dazzled by the brief flare of the match.

A glance in the mirror showed him the two men had

gone. Smart! They'd waited until the match briefly blinded him and then left, quickly and silently. It had to be by the side door. . . .

Cole crossed swiftly to a table where four townsmen were laughing over a joke one of them had just told. It was only a few feet from the side door.

'Two rannies just go out?' he asked and the laughter died slowly.

A big man in sweat-stained shirt, his chair facing the door nodded. 'Coupla strangers, Sheriff.'

'Blue shirt? Other with a vest over grey?'

The man was still nodding when Cole crossed to the door in two fast strides, then changed his mind and hurried down the smoke-filled room to the front batwings. He shouldered past a couple of men on their way in, ignoring the curses, moved quickly to the corner of the building.

There was no sign of his quarry in the now darkened alley. Darting his gaze about, he searched for places they might have gone. There were two lanes, one curving back to Front Street about a block along from the saloon. The other led to a secondary street, down past the general store, skirted the yard behind the saddler's and then swung towards the block where the bank stood.

And the side with the special door leading to Charlton's office faced onto it.

Cole drew his Colt, automatically checking the loads by turning the cylinder slowly and feeling the noses of the bullets in the chambers with his fingertip. While doing this, he watched for the men.

There was movement between him and the bank door, just a formless shadow, but it was too big to be that of a pariah dog or an alley cat. He padded forward, walking on the balls of his feet. It was a strain on his left leg but he gritted his teeth against the cramping pain. Only a few more steps and he would have the drop on them.

It was just a faint sound, very brief, as something whispered through the air. His reactions, he thought later, were as good as they had ever been, despite any residual hangover from that poisonous moonshine.

He propped and the descending gun clipped the brim of his hat. He lurched sideways as the man who had tried to drop him cold stumbled forward with the motion of the swinging weapon. Cole smashed his Colt into the side of the attacker's head, knocking off his hat. The man grunted and fell to the ground where his hat was already rolling in the dust.

His companion, near the bank door, heard the sounds and rounded fast, his gun firing, the flash briefly outlining him, clearly enough to show the faded blue colour of his shirt.

Cole triggered and his bullet knocked the man spinning. He crashed into the bank door, clawed at the wood and sat down, one leg bent under him. His head rested against the woodwork, his body jamming one arm. The other was clawing at his chest.

He froze when Cole's gun muzzle pressed into his grimy neck.

Just then a startled, eye-popping Linus Charlton wrenched open the door, gun in one hand, some banknotes in the other. 'What the devil. . . ?'

'Open the door wider, Linus. We've got two of 'em to drag in. With a little luck, it'll be an interesting conversation.'

'No!' The small-calibre handgun lifted and covered the surprised lawman. 'Sorry, Cole. No one comes into my office while I'm counting the ransom – and that includes you. If you want to question these two, take 'em down to your jail.'

The door slammed and the key turned in the lock.

The gunfire had attracted some curious folk, mostly drinkers from the saloon, and Cole organized four of them to bring the strangers down to the law office.

The wounded man was gasping that he needed a sawbones, he was dying.

'Then what you need is an undertaker,' Cole said flatly. 'You'll get medical attention in the cells. Fry, will you go get Doc Partridge and send him along?'

The townsman nodded and broke away from the small group following Cole. The man the sheriff gunwhipped was starting to groan and move a little but was still mighty groggy.

Until they reached the landing at the front door of the law office and Cole fumbled out his keys.

Then the man in the frayed vest suddenly came to life, kicking one of the men half-carrying him, smashing his forehead into the face of the second man, who lurched back, yelling, blood spraying. There was a tangle and Cole was knocked against the door, pinned briefly by the stumbling men.

Others were shouting but all dived for cover as the

man in the grey shirt pulled his gun and started shooting. A townsman dropped without a sound and another gave a cry of pain. The rest either hit the dirt or ran for whatever cover they could find.

The fugitive loosed two shots at Cole, making him duck. While the sheriff did that, trying to shoot past some of the weaving townsmen, the vest man leapt into the saddle of a horse at a nearby hitchrack and spurred away.

Cole jumped over prostrate townsmen, raised his Colt but swore as he was forced to hold his fire. The runaway was weaving in between the evening traffic and didn't offer a clear shot.

'Lock that *hombre* in the cell when the doc's finished with him,' he ordered as he started to run for a tethered horse. Pain immediately knifed through his leg and he staggered. But he was able to slap the reins loose and ram his left foot into the stirrup. His leg collapsed again and the horse whinnied and shied, throwing him.

Dimly, he heard the drumming of the other horse's hoofs as it sped over the bridge.

Cursing, a couple of townsmen helped get him into the saddle, ignoring yells from the horse's owner. He spurred after the fugitive, noting with satisfaction that there was a rifle in the saddle scabbard.

It was about as dark as it was going to get now and he had to rely on his ears to follow the escaping gunman. They were into the trees here, weaving between the trunks. Branches scraped his shoudlers as he lay low in the saddle. He reined down, the horse blowing, his heart slamming against his ribs. He couldn't hear the other mount!

Rifle in hand now, he eased the horse forward slowly, using his heels and knees to guide it; luckily it was a cow pony, used to such commands. Then flame stabbed out of the darkness to his right: *that son of a bitch had set up an ambush!*

The lead was close and he slid from the saddle, dancing on his good leg. He slapped the horse's rump, sending it racing on. The gun followed its sound, firing again.

Cole threw up the rifle, triggered at the flash, slightly up and to the left. He heard a grunt and a thrashing, and though he waited, there was no more shooting.

CHAPTER 8

CLOSING IN

'Am I gonna die, Doc?'

Partridge straightened and pressed one hand into his aching back, dropping bloody rags into a bucket on the cell floor.

'Well, I wouldn't say. . . .'

Cole, leaning against the end of the bunk in the cell, cleared his throat. The sound caught the doctor's attention and he paused. Cole shook his head slightly: *Don't tell him he's not going to die!*

Partridge knew what the lawman wanted from years of similar situations and turned again to the wounded man with the bandaged chest, stretched out on the bunk.

'I wouldn't say you were a good candidate for any long-term life insurance. Sorry, but I've done all I can.'

The man still had a black eye and a scabbed gash on his cheek from the fight with Cole on the Fourth of July. His skin was greyish and there was fear in his eyes. He pawed the doctor's arm as Partridge gathered his instruments and lotions.

'Doc, I – I can't breathe!' His chest was heaving but Partridge winked at Cole with the eye the wounded man couldn't see. He mouthed the word 'panic', but said aloud,

'Just lie quiet, son. It'll make the passing a lot easier. No sense in getting fussed at a time like this.'

'Oh, God!' The eyes were wide now, sought out the hard-faced Cole who was casually rolling a cigarette. 'I'm too young to die!'

'What are you? Twenty-four, twenty-five? Hell, I seen boys sixteen, *fourteen*, die in my squad durin' the War.'

'I'm twenny-six! An' I don't wanna die!'

Cole shrugged, held the cell door open for the medic to pass through into the passage. 'That's just what your pard said after I shot him in the trees earlier.'

From the passage, the doctor said, 'Best make a clean breast of your sins, son. Smoothe the way some. You'll feel better, with your conscience clear. I won't bother you with the undertaker right now. In the morning'll do.'

Partridge moved away down the passage and the wounded man rolled his head, began to cough, clasping his chest.

'What's your name?' Cole asked, as he finished making the cigarette and fumbled out a match.

'Larry Creed.'

'You like a last cigarette, Larry?' Cole held out the one he had just lit. 'Then again, guess it might tear up your lungs, and we're trying to make things easier for

83

you. But it's really up to you to help yourself.'

Creed stared, wide-eyed, mouth working soundlessly.

Cole, starting to turn away, suddenly swung back. 'You really want to unload yourself, Larry? Get some of your bad doings off your chest?'

Creed continued to stare, but when Cole shrugged and began to leave, he rasped, 'Wait up! Don't leave me to die alone.'

'Sorry, Larry. I've got a lot of paperwork to do. I'd like to oblige you, but I guess it's too late for that. I'll give you a little privacy. A man should take time to think about things when he's like you are, so close to goin'.'

'Er – no. I wouldn't mind you – stayin'. We could talk – for a bit.'

Cole frowned, looked uncertain. 'Well, I dunno. I've got a lot of things on my mind right now, too. Like Donny Charlton's kidnapping, and the ransom. I really don't think I can afford the time to just sit here and—'

'I – I can tell you somethin' about the kid.' Creed was eager, half-risen off the bunk now, convinced he would be dead before morning, wanting company right to the last.

'I don't even know who took him.'

'Aw, we got him. I mean me an' Mitch – my pard you just killed – and a coupla other fellers.'

'Tells me nothing. *Where?*'

'Well, we holed up in a crooked canyon in the Flintrocks.'

'That's a helluva big place, Larry!'

'Yeah – we just stumbled on the place. Damn good

hideout – almost at the base of the Church Spire. Know it?'

Cole did: it was a high column of basalt, tapering to a point like the spire on a church. He said nothing, drew on his cigarette, looking bored. Sitting on the edge of the bunk opposite Creed's, he moved restlessly, as if he was thinking of moving. Creed ran a tongue around his lips, his only thought that he didn't want to die alone; he was *eager* to talk so that Cole would stay put.

'Quinlan's behind it,' he gasped suddenly and the sheriff had to stop himself from revealing how interested he was in this piece of information.

'You're joshing me. I mean, what the hell would a man like Quinlan want to kidnap Donny Charlton for?'

Creed almost smiled. 'Got you interested now, huh? Well, Quinlan's havin' trouble with Devlin. Wants more money and Devlin won't cough up. So he got this idea of kidnappin' Charlton's brat. You know – a bank president, rich wife. They ought to be willin' to pay up, he figures. An' plenty.'

'Well, twenty thousand's sure a heap of money.' Cole hoped he spoke with the right amount of reverence.

Creed did smile now, not noticing any pain, having virtually forgotten his wound. 'Shucks – that's only the start!'

'What d'you mean?'

'They pay up, but Quinlan holds onto the kid – asks for another twenty thousand. You get it?'

Cole got it, all right. It was the kind of lousy deal Quinlan would pull. 'When's the ransom got to be paid? And how?'

'Ask Charlton. He's got all the details.'

Suddenly Creed narrowed his eyes, felt the bandages covering his chest wound. He rubbed them gently, frowned, staring at Cole. Then his face blackened as a thundercloud settled above it. *He wasn't feeling any worse!*

'Just a minute, you miserable son of a bitch. I ain't dyin' at all, am I! You and that stinkin' sawbones – you blame well *tricked* me! Judas priest—' His chest was heaving now with emotion. His words began to tumble over themselves, his anger so great he didn't finish all the syllables in one word before trying to spit out another.

'I've heard of fellers getting delirious just before they die, Larry. You best go easy. You're talking gibberish.'

'Christ, Cole! If I had a gun! A club! *Anythin'!* I'd pound your head flat!'

'Bet you would, too. Why'd you and Mitch come to Barberry? You bring another note?'

'Go ride off a cliff! I wish we'd kicked your face in at the hoedown!

'You seem to've recovered pretty well, Larry.' Cole dropped the cigarette and crushed it under a boot. 'Guess you ain't gonna tell me anything else, but I know a bit more now. You'll live to hang yet.'

Creed tried to struggle off the bunk as Cole unlocked the door and stepped out of the cell, but he *was* hurt, though far from fatally, and he sagged back, gasping. He swore savagely as the key turned in the lock.

'You – you ain't gettin' away with this, Cole, damn your eyes!'

'Maybe you better not kick up too big a fuss, Creed. If Quinlan gets to hear we got you prisoner, and *wounded* . . . Yeah, that's better. Relax. Someone'll bring you breakfast come morning. Now, get yourself a good night's sleep.'

Grating curses followed the sheriff all the way down to the front office.

'What the hell did Creed mean, saying you had all the details about paying the ransom, Linus?'

Cole glared down at the banker seated behind his desk, the piles of money covered with a green-baize cloth. Charlton looked highly nervous in the lamplight. He fiddled with the wick control, sat back, then immediately leaned forward and slopped some whiskey into a glass. He tossed it down, coughed once, looked hard at the sheriff.

'You want one, you'll have to drink from the bottle. I don't have another glass.'

'I don't want any, Linus – and you better quit. You make a mistake with your figures counting that money and you *will* be in a heap of trouble with your head office.'

It had taken a threat of blowing the lock off Linus's office door with a shotgun before the rattled banker would open up and allow the sheriff to enter.

'Creed says you know about paying the ransom. How? And I mean "how do you know"?'

Charlton started to reach for the bottle again,

changed his mind. He seemed to make a decision – or just remembered something. He reached into a desk drawer, waved a creased and grimy sheet of paper at Cole.

'I found this after I'd closed the side door on you earlier. Creed or Mitch must've pushed it under just before you jumped them.'

Cole frowned. Well, it sure wasn't Mitch – he was much too far away. But had Creed been close enough to push the note under the door? Hard to tell in the semi-dark, and then Mitch had tried to club him, and there was shooting. . . .

Cole took the paper and smoothed it on the banker's desk. He recognized the same printing as on the previous notes.

Tomorrow night. Right after moonset Birdwing Wells. North edge. Round rock broke on one side leave money under then get out we'll be watching If money OK kid'll be returned if not OK you only get part of him

Cole blew out his cheeks, looking at Linus as he downed another whiskey. 'Sounds like a Quinlan deal.'

Charlton started, suddenly wild-eyed. 'Quinlan? What's he got to do with it. . . ?'

Cole told him about Creed. 'Scared he was dying, didn't want me to leave, spilled his guts. Up to a point.'

'Oh, God! A man like Quinlan, holding Donny's life in his hands.'

'A man like what, Linus? You admitting you know Quinlan now?'

Linus slumped, nodded miserably. He held up his bandaged hand. 'He did this. A warning from Brack Devlin.'

'Guessed as much. But a warning about what?'

Linus stared blankly, then swallowed yet another drink. Cole leaned forward and took the bottle. The banker looked as if he would protest but changed his mind.

'Stay sober, you damn fool!'

Charlton slumped, not looking at the sheriff. He sighed heavily.

'All right. I'm something of a gambler on the quiet.'

'Not so quiet, Linus. I've known for months about your losses in Mannering's back room.'

This brought Linus's head up. His jaw dropped. 'You – you're full of surprises, Cole!'

'But you losing money to Mannering – how does that have anything to do with Brack Devlin?'

'They work for the same group back East. A group of hardheads own big pieces of their saloons, and a lot of others, I hear. Devlin's sort of a – a collector. He's told about who owes money—'

'And who's behind in paying up?'

Linus swallowed and nodded miserably. 'They think because I'm president of this bank I can lay my hands on money at any time! That's why they gave me so much easy credit. Damn fools! I have to account for every cent!'

'You're mighty foolish gambling at all in your position, Linus.'

'I've heard it all before, Cole! So don't waste your

breath.' The banker spoke tersely and then scrubbed a hand down his sweating face. 'I – I've tried to keep it from Bess. I hinted I needed some money but she's determined I'll never get my hands on a single dollar of her legacy.' He shook his head jerkily, compressed his lips. 'I could *kill* her at times! Anyway, to my surprise, after I explained to Mannering how I couldn't come up with what I owed right away, Quinlan suddenly appeared on my doorstep and made the most outrageous threats. All smiles and pleasant while he did so, which made them worse, if anything! Then he suddenly grabbed my left hand and – and broke my two middle fingers! I couldn't believe it was happening to me – in my own office! He clapped a hand over my mouth as I started to yell, banged my head back against the chair, then threw me on the floor and placed his boot across my throat. Still speaking calmly, he told me to either pay the money within one week or they'd find a way to make me pay up.'

'You didn't pay, so they kidnapped Donny and now demand twenty thousand in ransom. How much do you owe?'

'That's – that's none of your business, Cole!'

'I think it is, but let it go. You've been an awful damn fool, Linus. But I'll stick by my word and handle the ransom payment for you.'

For a moment he thought the rattled banker was going to cry but the man regained control, cleared his throat and looked longingly at the bottle in Cole's hands. The sheriff gave it to him and Linus drank straight from the neck.

'All right, Linus, let's get started and work out some kind of plan.'

'They've – already made the plan!'

'Their plan isn't necessarily mine.'

'Cole! You've got to do just as they say! Otherwise – you don't know what they'll do to Donny!'

'Or me if I ride in blind, hoping they'll stick to their side of things. It's all pretty damn risky, but I aim to come out of this alive, Linus.'

The banker put his head in his hands.

CHAPTER 9

OLD ENEMIES

Cole hired Josh and Joel Miller as temporary deputies, leaving them to watch the town – and Creed in the jail cell, with instructions to call Doc Partridge if necessary.

He hired a fresh mount from the livery, a strong-willed, hard-muscled black gelding with a wary eye and big, ready teeth.

'He'll run from here to next Tuesday week without falterin', long as you don't rake him with your spurs,' Earl the livery man assured Cole. 'Dig them rowels in too deep an' you'll be lookin' at the world from the top of the nearest tree – if he don't buck you clear over it.'

Cole must have looked uncertain, for the hostler added, 'I know you treat hosses OK, Cole. An' this one'll serve you well. My word on it.'

He also hired a packhorse, bought some supplies, including spare ammunition and shells for a sawn-off shotgun that came with the sheriff's job.

When he went to Linus Charlton's office to pick up

the ransom money he found the banker nervous and looking more than usually worried.

'It's not even noon, Cole! They said moonset, which won't be till after midnight.'

'I don't aim to keep to their timetable, Linus.'

'What the hell're you planning?'

'Just to arrive early and get the lie of things.'

'Damnit, Cole, don't you do anything that'll put Donny in danger!'

'Linus, he's already in danger. I won't take any chances of him coming to harm, but I don't aim to arrive in the dark. If I can, I'll save you that ransom money.'

Linus dropped into his desk chair, shaking his head, face white and sweating with strain. 'Will you please get it through your head that the *money's not important*! Let them have it! Just – just bring Donny back safely. I'm warning you, Cole, if anything happens to that boy because of you – well, I won't be answerable for your fate.'

Cole didn't smile, although Linus did seem a mite comical with his rotund figure, trying to bluster and sound tough. But the poor devil must be churning up inside, blood pressure off the scale, maybe not too far from a heart attack.

'Linus, you have my word I won't endanger Donny. Is the money ready?'

'Of course it's ready.' The banker went to his private wall safe in one corner of the office, opened it and brought out a scratched leather valise. It bulged and there was a twist of wire with a lead bank seal through

93

the strap and its buckle.

Cole frowned. 'I would've liked to've checked it myself, Linus. Don't look like that! I'm putting my life on the line to deliver it, and if there's been any mistake—'

'There is no mistake!' The banker was short of breath now, he waved a heavy arm as if brushing away a blue-tailed fly. 'Just go, Cole. I'm sorry if I seem unreasonable but I've never been under such a strain.' He glanced up with a mild twitch of his bloodless lips. 'I have this vision of Bess waiting to hear – with a large, razor-sharp knife in her hands, ready to emasculate me. . . .'

Poor devil: that woman had him whipped. Cole picked up the briefcase with one hand, noting its weight, and with the other clapped Linus briefly on his hunched shoulders.

'I should be back by sun up – with Donny.'

'I – I haven't prayed in years, but now I find myself constantly muttering a prayer that the kid'll be – all right.'

Charlton's haunted gaze stayed with Cole all the way back to where he had tethered his horses outside the law office.

Josh Miller came out onto the landing, watched him ram the valise under his warbag on the black. 'Luck, Cole.'

The sheriff nodded. 'Josh, you recollect what Donny was wearing at the Fourth's hoe-down? I wasn't tracking too well that day but I seem to recollect denim trousers and some sort of moccasins, and a cloth cap, but I can't get a picture of his shirt.'

'Kinda grey – he had that checked jacket of his to wear for the night show; maybe he had it on and you didn't notice the shirt. Oh, yeah, he give the jacket to young Sam Bale after he fell in the river, Sam havin' a bad cold an' all. Dunno if Donny had it on again when he went missin'.'

Mounted now, Cole nodded, lifted a hand briefly as Joel appeared beside his brother. They didn't look in the least alike except from behind: they both had red hair and the same-shaped head.

'Creed's complainin' he's dyin' again, Cole.'

'Might as well fetch the doc. But Creed's sneaky, so be careful going into the cell with him. *Adios*, boys.'

They watched him ride down Front, leading his pack-horse, and cross over the bridge. Then Joel started for Doc Partridge's and Josh went back into the cool of the office, starting to roll a cigarette.

Playing deputy was going to be a couple of days of easy money, he reckoned. A breeze.

Cole wasn't sure now whether he believed Larry Creed's story.

Quinlan *could* have set up the kidnapping off his own bat, but it was more likely that Brack Devlin had devised it as a way of recovering whatever money Linus owed Mannering, and, therefore, Devlin, as he was the Denver group's gambling controller for the area.

Linus was an utter fool for gambling when he was in such a position of trust. If ever there was a sum of money not accounted for at the bank, he would be

95

immediately under suspicion. He might think his superiors didn't know about his weakness, but Cole figured
those hard-nosed bankers would keep their fingers on
the pulse of all their branches – and the men who ran
them.

In any case, Quinlan was involved now, whether on
Devlin's orders or operating on his own. And he was a
mighty dangerous man, was 'Quick' Quinlan.

Cole had had a run-in with him about six months
back when he was working for Careful Carmody, driving
a freight wagon. Carmody was a twenty-mule-team man
from way back who had had enough savvy to change the
mules for four wheels and a six-horse team that could
be increased to eight if the load demanded it. The mule
teams had been too big an attraction for wandering
Indians, who saw the little animals only as food on the
hoof.

They were shipping-in gambling equipment for
Brack Devlin's new casino at the time: imported
roulette wheels, fancy card-tables with hidden slides
that could work in the house's favour with a little prac-
tice and know-how, dice tables, even a gilt-edged piano,
beds and ornate chairs; thousands of dollars' worth of
high-class fittings for the new gambling and pleasure
house.

Carmody's freight line had been free of raids by
Indians since doing away with the mule teams. But the
three wagons bound for Banjo Springs were close to
their destination when a bunch of tiswin-crazed braves
broke out of the new reservation at Greaswood Mesa.

The wagons lumbering across the wasteland, with

only two outriders, were too big a temptation to pass
up. The whole bunch, a round dozen in all, came
screaming out of the sun as the freighters whipped and
cursed their straining teams up the slope of a naked
hogback rise.

The big mistake the renegades made was not riding
around so they could attack coming *over* the rise, with
the wagons below them. Instead, minds still fogged with
tizwin fumes, they rode in across the flats, whooping
and screaming, and had to put their mounts up the
slope to reach the wagons.

Carmody, living up to his name, made no attempt to
try to outrun the raiders; a blind man could see that
would be futile. Instead, he signalled for the wagons to
turn across the slope, and when they did, managing it
just as the raiders came within gunshot range, the
outriders started shooting while the drivers grabbed
their guns.

Carmody had hired tough men, outriders and
drivers paid double because of their reputations with
firearms. Before the renegades could scatter, three of
them crashed off their mounts, two not moving again,
the third crawling away, trying to hold his stomach in;
he didn't crawl far.

The renegades were no doubt shocked and the rush
of adrenaline helped clear their brains. They scattered,
some riding up and around to get above the wagons.
Cole brought down two men and three horses with his
Winchester. Three got through and had the advantage
of shooting down into the wagons. The third driver, a
man named McLaren, was wounded badly in the chest,

but when a painted rider hauled alongside to climb aboard, McLaren shot him in the face with his six-gun. Bullets thudded into the wooden frames, and also into some of the merchandise. Even above the gunfire, Cole heard the new piano with the gingerbread gilt on the top give a loud, musical twang! as lead tore through the works. *Oh-oh!*

An outrider went down. Careful Carmody reeled as a bullet clipped one ear and blood sprayed from the mangled lobe. Cole had the heel shot off one boot but now the freighters were putting up such a withering fire with their repeating weapons that the surviving renegades, sobering by this time, lost their initial impetus and fell back, turned tail and limped away.

The wounded driver was attended to while Carmody examined the freight. He came back looking mighty worried.

'Devlin ain't gonna be happy,' was all he said, but a glance at the bullet-damaged freight was all that was needed to know that that was one hell of an understatement.

Brack Devlin was a smallish man with a narrow, hard face and deadly looking dark eyes. He was clean-shaven and always smelled of bay rum or some exotic male cologne. He dressed neatly and fastidiously, hair trimmed weekly just so, or there was hell to pay. He wore spectacles for reading, gold-wire frames, and he took them off when he heard the news about his freight – perhaps afraid his instant anger would steam up the lenses.

'You don't include the piano in the list of damaged goods, I trust, Carmody?'

The freighter, a beefy man and tough in his own right, nodded curtly, not afraid of Devlin, but uncomfortable at having to report such damage.

'Afraid so, Mr Devlin. Them renegades were lousy shots, and a lot of lead riddled my wagons.'

'Damn your wagons! I've been waiting for those goods for months! I've got prospective clients coming in from all over. Now you tell me my stuff is ruined!'

'Well, it sure is shot-up pretty bad, I have to admit, Mr Devlin, but I guess tradesmen could fix most of them things given time.'

'Oh, you do, huh? Where d'you think I'll find a piano tuner in this town? This *Territory*, for Chrissakes! Or a carpenter who can locate the same kind of wood for repairs? And who the hell is gonna pay for it!'

Carmody had been waiting for that; he brought out some folded sheets of paper from an inside jacket pocket. He shook desert dust from the papers as he smoothed them out.

'Well, this here's our contract, Mr Devlin, and you signed it. It says all goods carried at owner's risk, which means—'

'I know what it means, you son of a bitch! It means you think you're gonna stick me with the bill!'

'You can hardly blame me for a bunch of drunken Injuns—'

'You think not, huh? Well, you listen to me!' Brack Devlin yelled, rising out of his chair and leaning on his hands across the desk, face deep red. 'You're gonna pay the bill! No, don't try to worm outta this, Carmody! You weren't careful enough this time, not dealing with *me*! I trusted you to bring them things down from Denver and all you've delivered is a pile of junk!'

He was yelling really loudly now. The door opened quickly and Quinlan stepped in, one hand on his gun butt. He was like a barrel with legs, a *big* barrel, and his head rested on top of wide shoulders like a balanced cannon ball. He had jet-black sideburns, and his curly black hair came low on his forehead. Bushy eyebrows jutted above deep sockets and cold brown eyes stared out like gun barrels.

Well-trained, eager for violence, Quinlan headed straight for the freighter, coming in like a bull buffalo.

Careful Carmody grew careless, tried to ease his six-gun out of leather on the side away from the man. Quinlan towered over him, and slammed *his* Colt barrel across the freighter's head. The big man caught him easily as his legs folded, heaved him over one shoulder, turned to look at the fuming Devlin.

'What about his crew?'

'You know what to do. Now go and do it. And burn the bastard's wagons for good measure. If I'm not going to get dollar-one outta him, I'll see him ruined as well as crippled by the time I'm through.'

Quinlan grinned in anticipation and strode towards the door. . . .

Cole had been at the livery, arranging corral space for the teams, and now headed back to the freight depot, crossing a vacant lot and coming up on it from the rear.

He almost stumbled over the body of the other driver – the wounded one was at the local infirmary – sprawled in the long grass. The man was a mess, face barely visible behind a mask of blood, nose obviously broken, one ear torn, jaw hanging slackly which likely meant it, too, was broken. His shirt was ripped and blood-streaked flesh showed through the rent, also some mud and grit: sure signs he had been kicked repeatedly.

Hand on gun butt now, Cole rose from his knees on hearing a muffled cry. He saw scuffling figures down by the harness shed. A huge man was beating up on Careful Carmody. The freighter's legs would no longer hold him but he was supported between two men, all three jarring as Quinlan hammered his big fists into the already unconscious man. As Cole ran forward, they released Carmody and Quinlan glanced over his shoulder, snapped at the two hardcases,

'Take care of him.'

Then he proceeded to kick and stomp the downed freighter. Cole slowed, not believing his eyes for a moment. Then the two hardcases rushed him. He was in no mood for fair play here. He drew his gun – later the men swore they never even saw his right arm move – and fired twice. Both men fell, wounded through the upper legs, writhing and moaning in bloody agony.

The shots brought Quinlan spinning, and for a large man he moved mighty fast. He was breathing hard as he lifted his Colt and Cole stepped in, slammed his own gun down across the man's thick wrist. The six-gun fell and Quinlan grunted, grabbing at his wrist, but he curled thick lips and spat at Cole.

Next instant, Quinlan's vast bulk was slammed up against the shed hard enough to rattle the planks. Some harness on nails inside was jarred loose and fell, jingling.

Then Cole's smoking gun barrel moved in a blur, slamming from side to side, half a dozen times in the blink of an eye. The foresight ripped up Quinlan's face and his thick legs started to fold under him. Blood streaked across his cheeks, his nose lay over to one side, spurting thick streams of blood, one eyebrow was torn loose and his lips were cut from broken teeth. Cole lifted a knee into his crotch and Quinlan fell forward, hitting the ground in a huddled ball, barely conscious. Cole gave him one savage kick, then holstered his gun and knelt beside the bloody, disfigured Carmody.

The freighter was in terrible shape with many broken bones and for a moment there Cole almost put a bullet into Quinlan. But he figured the big man had been marked for life.The word would soon spread about how he had come by such a marked-up face. (Quinlan grew a beard to hide the scars, later on. Though his inner scars were burning for revenge.)

'Maybe I should've killed him,' Cole murmured now as he rode towards his rendezvous with the ransom money. 'He's gonna do his best to kill me some day.'

But even though Quinlan was badly hurt, his wounds and their aftermath were nowhere near as bad as those inflicted upon Careful Carmody. The freighter would never be the same again, spoke vaguely, didn't recognize many of his old friends these days, could only get around on crutches.

Cole had heard several times that Quinlan had vowed Cole would need a wheelchair when they had their inevitable reckoning. But, strangely, Devlin wouldn't allow Quinlan to go after Cole.

'The man's a lawman now, duly sworn and with Denver's approval. Kill him and we'll have marshals coming out of the woodwork, poking their noses into our affairs where we don't want 'em. Leave him be for now. We'll find a way to fix the sonuver when we're good and ready.'

Now, suddenly, Cole wondered for one fleeting moment, if maybe they had found that way – getting him out here alone, carrying twenty thousand dollars.

CHAPTER 10

RECEPTION

The ransom was to be paid at Birdwing Wells, but Larry Creed had inferred the boy was still being held in the crooked canyon near the Church Spire rock.

The places were miles apart and the fact that the ransom was to be paid over in the middle of the night – well, it seemed mighty suspect to Cole.

It smelled of a set-up. And if that was what it was, Quinlan was bound to be involved.

But there had been nothing in any of the ransom notes naming Cole as the one to deliver the ransom money. Linus had asked him as a personal favour; in any case, Cole felt it was his bounden duty to take on the job: he still felt responible for Donny Charlton's abduction.

They couldn't have known ahead of time that he would be the one to make the delivery; in fact, there was a good chance they still didn't know *who* was bringing the money.

He couldn't work it out satisfactorily; maybe they planned to kill *whoever* brought the ransom. That way they would avoid being recognized or tied in with the kidnapping. They would realize that there would be a hue and cry afterwards. Bess Charlton would see to that, even if Linus didn't.

That was if they didn't kill the kid anyway, which was the only really safe way for kidnappers. Remove *all* chance of identification, starting with the abducted person, and whoever paid over the ransom, just to be sure.

He wasn't about to risk his neck by riding in blindly, following the instructions in the note to the letter. There was no room for improvisation or changes of direction: *right after moonset, leave the money under the round rock with one side sheared off, north side of the wells.*

That meant being in a certain place, at a certain time, close enough to reach the deposit rock by deadline.

A perfect plan for dry-gulching. They would know where he was at any given time after he passed the point that would allow him to reach the rock right after moonset.

Like hell!

It was late afternoon when he rode close to the hills, using the creeping shadows to make him hard to see. He had deliberately chosen the black mount and a dark-coloured packhorse so they would be hard to distinguish at night or in deep shadows around sundown. He wore dark clothing for the same reason.

He had brought a map with him, although he had

been out here once before, looking for a horse-thief; he'd found him in a ravine, dead, the equally dead horse lying on top of him at the base of a cliff. It was dangerous country and Cole figured to get within a frog's leap of the Birdwing Wells while there was still light enough to see.

Which meant that anyone holed up with a rifle would be able to see him coming, too. But there was no avoiding it. He had studied the map closely and worked out a trail that would give him reasonable cover. Not that that meant much: if they were going to dry-gulch him, they would have all approaches under surveillance.

But, with the few facts he had, it was the best he could do. He rode with his rifle unsheathed, the butt resting on his right thigh; they would expect him to take precautions, so would shoot first, without warning.

This was country with lots of broken rock, crags jutting and hanging, making good lookouts for anyone wanting to see who was riding below, yet keeping hidden.

There were lots of shadows, deep black against the pale rock, but, at this time, there were still patches of sunlight that he was unable to avoid. His flesh crawled when he crossed these, eyes raking the heights, finger on the rifle trigger. He tensed at a flickering movement up there, relaxed almost immediately when he realized it was only a baby eagle, not yet ready to fly, flapping in a stick nest. While he watched the bird's antics, looking out for the homing mother with food, he caught another movement out of the corner of his left eye. It was on a neighbouring jutting crag, some twenty feet down from the rim.

That was no bird. It was a man changing position, likely growing cramped on the narrow ledge. A slanting shaft of sunlight flashed back at him from a rifle barrel.

Cole turned the black and the packhorse under a ledge and dismounted. He crouched in front of the big horse, certain he had not been seen by the watcher. The man was in the right place for an ambush, having a good view of the trail where it came out of a narrow, winding section. But he wouldn't be able to see the rider *in* that section, only when he reached the end and appeared in the open below the ledge.

He called up a picture of his map in his mind, relating the position of the ledge to where he knew Birdwing Wells lay ahead. Glancing at the sky, he smiled thinly: yeah! The sun was behind the hills now, throwing sawtoothed shadows in long, distorted patterns, misty rays fanning above the crags.

They would expect him to appear here just after sundown. That would still give him time to make his way carefully through the high ranges to the wells – where he could hole up until the moon set, and be ready to look for the broken rock and leave the ransom.

He figured he wasn't meant to ride out again.

But he had a plan to change that.

The first thing he did was hide the ransom in the bottom of a crevice, covering it with smaller rocks. The brown packhorse was docile, obedient, long used to obeying commands of men. Cole off-loaded the packs, took out his bedroll, and searched for and found a

107

reasonably straight branch about three feet long, fallen from a tree that had long ago been struck by lightning. It was still strong and he broke off some of the thin, projecting branches, rammed the remaining shaft through his bedroll, end to end. He stood this vertically on his saddle, tied it in place with his lariat to saddle-horn and cantle. It was unsteady but would suffice. He hung a threadbare denim jacket over the top and jammed his hat on to hold it in place.

It would never pass in daylight, but in the shadows of a winding narrow trail through these hills it would look enough like a man to hold a watcher's attention. He hoped that the packhorse, once started, would auto-matically keep going, following the winding trail. He gave it a handful of oats, scratched it behind one ear. It nuzzled him and he stroked the muzzle, then stepped to the rear, slapping a hand across the rump.

The horse snorted a little but jerked forward and started along the deeply shadowed trail.

He glanced up between the towering walls and through the jagged slit they made against the darken-ing sky, saw the first faint stars. The three-quarter moon that had been hanging above the range all day began to glow as the light faded, fast now.

Hatless, he mounted, rifle in hand, and turned the black around, riding out of the broken entrance. He put the horse parallel with the rising hills, moving roughly in the same direction as the packhorse with its strange rig – and hoping it would hold and not topple from the saddle.

There was more light here and he was able to travel

faster, but kept the black on softer ground where he could. He had worked out from his map where he should dismount and go in on foot, had climbed up a high rock for a better view and noted a lone pine tree about level with the position where he had seen the rifleman.

When he reached the tree he dismounted and tied the black to the trunk. He made a last check of his six-gun and rifle magazine, put a handful of spare shells in his shirt pocket, and ran back to the first slope of the hills. He began to make his way up. His game leg took the strain all right, but he moved cautiously. Stars were twinkling brightly above now. The moon was like a lantern washing the slopes with pale light – just enough to throw shadows over the twisting trail travelled by the packhorse. Sweat prickled him as the slope steepened and in two places he had to slide the rifle barrel through his belt at the back and use both hands to climb. He was breathing hard, trying not to snort too loudly.

His heart thudded against his ribs when he reached the place he had estimated would be level with the dry-gulcher's position. He paused, heaving deep breaths, steadying himself, then, after quietly levering a shell into the breech, he clambered over the rock.

He had guessed well. There was the ledge below and to his right, with the man stretched out, his upper body rising a little so he could better see down to where the narrow trail opened onto the sandy area below.

The ambusher settled back, brought his rifle up to his shoulder. Cole heard the lever work, then, in the silence, the clip-clop of the slowly moving packhorse below.

Cole eased forward, swore softly as the movement sent a handful of gravel spilling over the edge. It pattered across the legs of the man below and he spun onto his back. Cole dropped. There was a startled curse from the rifleman as he tried to roll aside and at the same time bring his gun around. The brass butt plate scraped across the ground. He almost had the weapon in position to shoot when Cole's body landed beside him. Cole threw himself across the man, jamming the hand holding the Winchester against a rock. He slammed it hard and the gun clattered. The man drew up his knees and kicked at Cole's belly.

One boot took him on the hip – the wounded one – and searing pain drove through him. Fuelled by the agony, he smashed his forehead into the other's face, felt nose and lips mash. Cole reared to his knees and slammed the rifle butt savagely across the ambusher's head. The body beneath him went limp.

Cole sat back, gasping, massaging his throbbing hip, hoping the rest of the reception committee weren't close enough to have heard the scuffle.

When the thwarted bushwhacker came round, he found he was bound hand and foot and his own neckerchief had been wadded up and pushed into his mouth to gag him.

He could hardly breathe through his nose: it was clogged with blood, but there was something hard blocking his left nostril as well. It hurt when he twitched his nose and he looked up with wide, puzzled eyes at Cole sitting on a nearby rock.

There was enough light for them to make out each other's features and Cole leaned forward, fumbled a match out of his shirt pocket. He held it up in front of the now thoroughly scared prisoner, thumbnail against the match-head, ready to snap it into flame.

'Just gonna say this once, *amigo*. What you've got stuck up your nostril is a bunch of four vestas, just like this one. I flick my thumbnail and it lights up. I move it closer to its pards hanging out of your nose and . . .' He stopped speaking, shrugged. 'You're dumb but I reckon you got enough brains to figure out what'll happen. And you can see why I'll only ask you just once what I want to know. You won't have a second chance. OK?'

The man was grunting endlessly, trying to speak, squirming in terror.

'Take it easy. What I'm gonna ask you is how many of your pards are waiting at Birdwing? When I ask, you nod if you're gonna tell me and I'll take that as your word you won't make a noise. If you break your word. . . .'

The man was nodding frantically, bulging eyes fixed on the match only inches from his face: he understood all too well.

'OK. Consider the question asked. Now, do I light this or . . . Ah! You want to talk? Uh-huh. Now make sure you savvy what I want you to do . . .' More frantic nodding and whining sounds. 'Here we go, then.'

Still holding the threatening vesta close to the

battered face, Cole tore the wadded, saliva-wet kerchief from the man's mouth. The prisoner coughed and gagged, spat.

'I'm waiting!' Cole said impatiently.

'Thr . . . three. Quinlan insisted – on – comin' his – hisself.'

'Quinlan! So,that snake *is* behind it. All right, friend. One more question: have they got the kid with them?'

Panic-stricken eyes stared and Cole sighed, lifted his thumb, ready for the thumbnail strike against the match. Sweat struck his face as the prisoner quickly shook his head.

'No!'

'Not so damn loud! Where is he?'

'In – in some canyon Creed found earlier.'

'OK, friend. I know where it is.'

'What – what you gonna do with me?'

Cole put his vesta back in his pocket and reached for the ones still jammed in the man's nostril. Suddenly, with the immediate threat gone, the man stupidly lunged at Cole, hands and feet bound, trying to ram the top of his head into Cole's face, using his weight in an attempt to knock him over the ledge.

The sheriff dodged to one side, slipped and sprawled. There was a brief yell and a clatter of falling rocks as the bound man hurtled off the ledge. He crashed head first down to the clear area below where the packhorse waited patiently, its fake 'rider' having slid all over to one side, and was now minus the hat.

Cole looked down, but his prisoner wasn't moving:

his head was twisted at an odd angle, a spreading stain darkening the shale underneath.

Well, that solved one problem, anyway,

CHAPTER 11

CHURCH SPIRE ROCK

It was deathly quiet at Birdwing Wells. Not even a single insect buzzed or hummed or whined.

The moon was low down, sliding behind the bulk of the mountain, balancing on the crest briefly, then dropping gradually until it was hidden from sight. The glow still outlined the crest but slowly faded and a solid darkness claimed the slopes. The stars blazed coldly and shed a meagre light, but nothing could be seen to move.

Then there was a sound: a slight rasping of cloth as someone hidden in the rocks facing the north side of the wells changed position.

'Sit still, damn you!' hissed a deep voice and there was discernible anger in the few words.

'I hear him!' another voice said in hushed tones.

And then came the soft, cautious *plop* of a horse

114

making its way to the water where the stars were reflected.

'He's not s'posed to—'

'*Christ!*' growled Quinlan in exasperation. His rifle came up as he glimpsed the shadowy outline of the rider on the slow-moving horse below.

The Winchester's crashing shots tore the night apart, slammed back from the rising rock walls, the sound intensifying as the other guns blazed.

The rider below was blown out of the saddle as the horse whinnied and reared, jerking away. It ran, dragging the body for several yards before it fell completely clear.

'Stop the goddamn hoss! It'll be carrying the ransom!'

Two rifles hammered and the horse whickered, reared, stumbled, and then slid down the slope to come to rest at the edge of the water, which rippled violently, shattering the stars' reflections.

Three men slid and lurched their way down the slope, all making for the fallen horse.

'Check Cole!' Quinlan snapped at one man who swore under his breath as he veered away and crossed to where the rider was sprawled face down.

Quinlan and the third man came upon the horse which was quivering its last. At a sign from Quinlan the other man began searching for the saddlebags which were jammed underneath.

The man upslope ripped out an oath. Quinlan spun. 'What. . . ?'

'This ain't Cole. It's Smitty! Looks like he fell off a cliff.'

Quinlan's huge bulk climbed up the slope and he looked down at the battered body of the man who had been left to cover the trail to the wells – and to cut off Cole's retreat.

'Son of a *bitch*!' Quinlan's deep voice thundered across Birdwing Wells. 'He killed Smitty and roped him to the saddle! Now, where the hell is he?'

'Gone after the kid, I reckon. Smitty never did have much guts. He'd talk if Cole went to work on him.'

The man examining the empty saddlebags stood up and put in his two cents' worth:

'He'll have a damn good start! All the time we been waitin', thinkin' it was him comin' along that narrow trail—'

'Go get the horses!' growled Quinlan, at the same time cursing. He had been the one who insisted they leave the mounts at least half a mile away in a small wash, blocked off with brush, in case the animals sensed the lone rider's mount approaching the wells and whinnied, giving away their presence.

Now they would lose more time collecting the damn horses! And every minute, Cole was moving away from them – closing in on the Church Spire canyon where two more men had the kid.

'He won't get past Rooster or Blackie, Quick,' said the man who had examined the body, trying to sound reassuring.

'He better not,' gritted Quinlan, kicking the ground in his frustration. *'Now get the goddamn horses!'*

Cole was sorry he had had to sacrifice the packhorse –

116

it had been obedient and uncomplaining – but it was necessary. He'd recovered his bedroll and replaced it with the dead man from up on the ledge, roping him in the saddle.

At best it was only a delaying action, but every minute he could confound Quinlan and whoever was with him was a bonus.

He knew the way to Church Spire Rock and even in the now moonless night he rode at a good clip. The black was strong and fast, actually ready to run a lot faster than Cole was allowing it to, but he was leery of the horse's strength. Some of these big, muscular stallions and geldings once they cut loose took a lot of stopping.

He was careful to keep the spur rowels away from the black and when he came out of the tangle of gulches and hills where the Birdwings were, he put the mount across the grassy flats until they ran into dusty ground, then he slowed again. The horse was not pleased, turning its head and taking a half-hearted snap at his left leg.

'Yeah, I know. If you had the chance, you'd chomp me good. I savvy your frustration.'

The horse wanted to run again, eager for the exercise, but now was the time to go into those canyons at a wary pace. Starlight was not very helpful in there with the high walls and narrow passages. He found himself all tensed up, mouth dry, belly muscles hard, hand gripping the rifle until his bones ached.

He was over-confident at one stage, became lost and thought for a time it would be damned near daylight

117

before he found a way out of the tangle of canyons and dead ends he had ridden into.

But he spooked a cougar feeding on a deer it had downed and the animal had taken off. A glimpse of it silhoutted against the stars told him it was a female, heavily pregnant, which probably explained its willingness to flee – even wild cats had a powerful mother-instinct to make sure no harm came to the babies.

But the cat had shown him the way out of the scrambled knot of gulches: minutes later, he saw the spired rock rearing against the stars. He was closer than he had expected and now he dismounted and led the black by the reins up the first slopes of the mountain that hid the crooked, winding canyon Larry Creed had spoken of. Surprisingly, the black came willingly and it was not difficult to lead it through scattered rocks so that its hoofs did not disturb them.

When he reached the top and the downslope fell away into the start of the canyon, Cole pushed the rifle back into the saddle scabbard, punched in the top of his hat and filled it with water from his canteen. The black slurped it up, then Cole took the sawn-off shotgun from the left hand saddlebag and a handful of shells from his pocket. He broke the gun and thumbed home two loads, but did not close the action fully: there was no safety and this was the only way he could make sure the gun wouldn't accidentally discharge if he stumbled or fell.

It was a long, snaking canyon and he had no idea where Creed's pards had holed up. It was a safe bet that it would be somewhere high on the slopes, so they could keep an eye on the approaches. This meant he had to travel slowly and watch both sides, hoping for some sign of a camp, but he figured they would have it well hidden.

The horse was growing restless now, had rested enough and was eager to be running again, cutting an exhilarating passage through the wind. The hoofs clattered a couple of times, freezing Cole in his tracks, ears straining.

The black was beginning to assert itself now, tugged at the reins, almost pulling him off balance. He stumbled, just managed to hold his tight grip on the shotgun, cursed the big animal.

'Damn you! I should've run you till you couldn't stand! Now, behave, goddammit!'

His efforts were puny against the strength of the horse, which was enjoying itself now, straining back with arched neck, keeping the reins taut so Cole couldn't get any slack, the leather starting to slide inexorably through his hands.

He suddenly let go and the horse stumbled, forefeet crossing as it tried to find solid footing after the unexpected release of pressure. In a flash, Cole was in the saddle, had the reins taut, throwing his weight back, the bit hard against the back of the black's mouth. Surprisingly, it accomodated his movements, settled, standing four-square solid now, head up, as if eagerly awaiting Cole's command.

He almost made the mistake of touching the spurs to the sweating flanks. But he stopped in time, settled the shotgun across his legs and flicked the reins.

'You're a playful devil, ain't you? Just like to let me know who's really in charge. OK, we go up, at an angle towards that. . . .' Cole stood in the stirrups, staring unbelievingly.

There was a red spark up there, this side of the crest, at least twenty feet below. *A red spark* – that could only be coals of a banked campfire, or one that hadn't been fully extinguished earlier. The black's antics had occurred over a considerable area of ground, taken them more than halfway through the winding canyon.

That had to be Creed's cronies' camp, maybe outside a cave or overhang of rock. He couldn't risk the black's deciding to put on another demonstration of its independence, so he ground-hitched the horse. He could see the animal wasn't pleased.

'You stay put and be ready to carry me, and, hopefully, a young boy not more'n forty-fifty pounds. . . .'

He patted the muzzle and almost had his hand bitten. He smiled ruefully and started up the slope. It was awkward carrying the shotgun, but he had figured it for the best weapon to use in the confines of the canyons.

The slope was steeper than it looked and he had to make his progress in a series of slow zigzags across. His breath burned the back of his throat with his efforts and the wounded leg was acting up, aching, not as strong as it had been originally. It gave way unexpectedly and, leaning forward, he had to put down a hand to keep from falling.

It saved his life.

A rifle crashed not five yards above and he heard the

ripping sounds of the bullets passing over his back. He dropped and rolled now, snapping the shotgun closed, coming over onto his belly. The gun flashed above him again and the bullet kicked stones and dirt against his side.

Then the shotgun thundered and he glimpsed the dark shape of the guard up there, doubled over as if kicked in the belly by a cranky mustang. The man gave a strangled croak and fell forward, rolling part-way down the slope.

'Rooster!' someone called from a deeper black patch above the coals of the campfire, which he could see now. 'Who the hell is that?'

If the man expected an answer he was disappointed. Cole could make out the entrance to a cave now and the man lurched out, rifle butt braced against his hip, lever working as he fired again and again, raking the slope.

Cole spun away to one side and while still on his left side, triggered the shotgun's second barrel. The gunman staggered as if he had hit a wall, but he wasn't about to give up.

He took a couple more steps, getting off two wild shots, the last one pointing to the ground. Cole dropped the shotgun, palmed up his Colt and fired once.

The man fell, rolling and sliding down past Cole, the rifle clattering after him.

Cole ignored him, started up the slope, hoping there *had* been only two guards. Crouching by the cave entrance, he called warily,

121

'Donny? Donny? You in there?'

No answer, but someone coughed deep inside the cave.

'It's Sheriff Cole, Donny. Are you OK?'

'I – I'm OK, Sher'ff,' called a shaky, thin voice from back in the darkness. 'Only – I ain't Donny. I'm Sam Bale.'

CHAPTER 12

HOME ON THE RANGE

The kid was a mess. He was still wearing Donny Charlton's jacket but it was stained with mud and red rock dust, the seam was torn on one shoulder and a pocket was starting to break away.

He had a black eye and his face was smeared with dirt. Large front teeth and freckles, a formless kid's nose and eyebrows that were barely discernible – this was Sammy Bale. His hair was tow-coloured like Donny's, but there must be at least another dozen boys of varying ages in town with the same colour hair.

Cole could see how simple it would be for the kidnappers to make a mistake: likely they had been cowboys or hardcases hired for the abduction and not actually knowing Donny Charlton by sight; they would have been told to look for a tow-haired seven-year-old, probably wearing a reasonably new jacket if it was in the cool of evening near the start of the night-time fire-works' show.

Sammy Bale had a heavy cold; he was sniffling and coughing occasionally even as Cole cleaned him up and gave him some food, It was obvious from the way Sam ate that he hadn't been fed much lately.

'What happened, Sam?'

The boy swallowed the last of his fifth corn dodger, wiped the back of a wrist across his mouth and started to use the same wrist on his moist nostrils. Cole stopped him, gave him a kerchief. Sam blew into it and offered it back. Cole lifted a hand.

'Consider it a gift, Sam. Now tell me how come you were snatched instead of Donny?'

'I dunno. I mean, I fell in the river and Donny pulled me out and I was shiverin' with this cold an' he give me his new jacket to wear.' The boy's bright-blue eyes lit up. 'It's a beauty. I wish it was mine.'

'You ask Donny could you keep it on?'

'Sort of.' He hung his head a little, watching Cole's face from under his thin eyebrows. 'I – I said I was still cold and put on a bit of a wheeze or two. Donny said I could keep it on but I'd have to give it back when his ma showed up. She's kinda – snooty, Donny's ma, you know?'

'Haven't had much to do with her but I got that impression.'

Sam gave a quick smile, glad to have Cole agree with him. 'Anyway, we was scavengin' around for some spare rockets and these two fellers come up and said they had found three or four unfired ones. We started to go with

124

'em, but one grabbed Donny by the arm and lifted him clear off the ground, carried him off somewhere behind a wagon. I got scared and tried to run but I tripped and I hit my head.' He pulled his hair back and a bruise and slight swelling were still obvious. 'I was knocked out, I guess. When I come round I'm lyin' over this dark feller's lap on his hoss with my wrists tied behind my back. They brought me to this cave an' I been here ever since.'

'Know who the man was?'

'Rooster – the first one you killed. The other was Blackie someone.'

Cole rolled a cigarette, lit up and smoked thought-fully. Sam started eating again.

'Not too much, too fast. If your belly's been starved for a few days, you go easy.'

Sam looked as if he would argue but then thought better of it, wiped his hands down the front of the stained jacket.

'Donny's ma'll throw a fit when she sees this.'

'Yeah, could be. I'm wondering what happened to Donny. Everyone's convinced he was the one kidnapped. And how come your ma didn't raise hell when you went missing?'

'Aw – I dunno.' Small shoulders shrugged; he didn't seem unduly worried that his mother hadn't reported him missing. He wouldn't meet Cole's gaze.

'You been running off from home now and again?' Cole asked suddenly and the way Sam jumped and moved a little away from him gave him his answer. 'You been skedaddling off for so long that your ma's gotten

125

used to it, no longer bothers if you don't show up till you're good and ready. That it?'

Cole's voice had anger in it and the boy started to cringe, head on one side as if expecting a cuff. Cole immediately relented.

'Hey, boy, don't do that! I ain't gonna hit you. Is that why you run away every now and again? Because your ma whips you?'

'She don't, but he does sometimes when he's been at the likker.'

'Who's "he"?'

Sam took his time answering, pulled some grass and tore up the blades one by one as he spoke, eyes downcast.

'Well, sir, my ma – she never been married, see?' He waited, challengingly, but Cole's face remained blank. 'My pa was killed before he could marry her and she said she never wanted no other man for a husband. . . .'

'It's OK, Sam. I understand. She feels the need now and again for a man's company, is that it?'

Sam looked relieved and smiled briefly. 'I guess. But this feller, this Winston, says he's my uncle. He's been hangin' around, don't seem to wanna leave. I know Ma *wants* to get rid of him but he's sort of – taken over. She told me we'd run off if the farm wasn't all she had in the world, and she wants to keep it – for me.'

There was a hint of tears in the boy's eyes and voice now. He paused, gulping.

'Sam, your ma sounds like a good woman to me. But we've got to get outta here before some other men involved in your kidnapping turn up. And I've got to

126

find Donny Charlton! You any idea where the hell he could be?'

Sam didn't and Cole figured it was time they were somewhere else. He stood, dropped the cigarette butt and crushed it.

'C'mon, kid. I'll take you home.'

'Where the hell is he goin'?' Red Carlin snapped irritably as Quinlan led the way down the dark slope. 'Would be better if the damn moon was still out.'

'Be a whole *lot* better if you kept your mouth shut!' Quinlan growled.

'We ain't gonna pick up any trail in the dark, Quick,' said the third man, Smoky Hill, trying to sound reasonable. No one wanted to stir Quinlan's temper; when the man was crazy mad he didn't differentiate between friend and foe.

'Where d'you think he's going?' Quinlan asked, his deep voice rasping. 'He's gonna take the kid back home, for Chrissakes.'

There was silence and, riding side by side, Red and Smoky exchanged a glance, or as much of one as each could see in the dark.

'Quick,' Red said, licking his lips. 'We heard his hoss while gettin' our own mounts, and it wasn't goin' back towards Barberry.'

'That's a fact, Quick,' added Smoky quietly.

Quinlan reined down, yanking the reins so hard his mount snorted and pranced in protest.

'Is that right? Well, he had to find his way outta the canyon, didn't he? It twists and turns like a snake with

127

colic. *After* he clears it is where we'll pick up his proper trail. It ought to be light enough then, and it'll lead back to Barberry. Don't make sense any other way.'

Smoky and Red were silent, then Smoky leaned out and nudged Red's leg, urging him by nods of his head to speak up. After a few moments he heard Red clear his throat.

'Quick, he could be makin' his way back to the Bale farm.' Quinlan snapped his head up and Red added, quickly, 'All along that kid reckoned he was Sammy Bale, not the Charlton brat.'

'Little swine was just actin' up ornery,' Quinlan said, harshly. '*D. Charlton* was sewed into the collar of the coat he was wearing. He was just trying to be smart so's we'd let him go.'

Red sighed, glanced at Smoky for some back-up but Hill remained quiet. Red swore softly; now he was left alone to argue with Quinlan and he didn't know too many men who'd won such a contest. Didn't know any! But he had spoken now and had to back up his reasoning.

'He had a good explanation for the coat, Quick. The Charlton kid lendin' it to him after he fell in the river, 'cause he had a cold – and you can't deny he sure does have a bad cold, snotty-nosed little hellion.'

'Red, I'm convinced we had Donny or Danny Charlton, whatever the hell his name is. But, as I said, it'll be light enough to read Cole's tracks soon. *Then* we decide which way we go. Now, that's it! Both of you shut up till we get outta these damn canyons!'

Red and Smoky were glad to obey.

Mattie Bale was in her late twenties, quite good-looking, though careworn from long years of hard work and worry about everyday living. The farm wasn't large but it was a lot of work for one woman, with only the occasional help of an active eight-year-old boy, when she could nail him down for long enough.

She had actually been glad when Winston Bale had turned up, brother of Steven, Sammy's father. He had been obliging enough at first, pitching in, making the place more like a farm should be – and then he moved into her bed.

'I'd be your brother-in-law if Steve hadn't been killed and you know a man's brother can claim his rights from his sister-in-law when she's widowed.'

'That's not a law!' she argued. 'It's what some folk want to believe, is all.'

He was a handsome man, Winston. His smile had won him many a throbbing female heart since he was in his teens. He always had his way with women – always. And Mattie would be no different. 'Well, *I* believe it,' he told her, flashing that smile. 'I surely do.'

And, in the end, the smile worked for him once again.

But his original eagerness to work and build up the farm had its edge blunted soon after and he spent a lot of time lounging around the cabin, or fishing down at the creek. He was good to Sammy, took him fishing with him, but didn't care whether it was a school day or not and Sammy lost a deal of education. And he didn't mind boxing the boy's ears when Sam annoyed him in some way, either.

Mattie found she was working harder than ever now there were three of them – tending her vegetable patch, trapping rabbits and possums and squirrels and other small game just to put meat on the table. Once or twice Winston brought in a fish big enough to share, and one time he actually hunted down and killed a deer.

But mostly he did little around the farm and began to boss both Mattie and Sammy: 'Time to milk the cow, boy. Get it done.' 'Go collect some more eggs from the chicken pen Mattie, I fancy a big omelette for my lunch.' 'Go into town and bring me back some fresh tobacco – oh, and a bottle of Mannering's rye – he'll give you credit.'

'I *hate* going near that saloon,' Mattie complained and his dark eyes narrowed.

'You do what I say, woman! And tell Judd Reason I want to see him, too.'

She stiffened when he said that. 'Why d'you want to see that snide land dealer?'

'Why d'you just ask for a smack in the mouth by givin' me an argument! *You do what I say!*'

She knew what he was about: he was negotiating the sale of the farm, somehow going to fix it with Judd Reason, although the farm title was in her name. But Winston Bale had some way around that, and she knew she and Sammy wouldn't see any money from such a sale.

130

But it never came to that, for Winston devised a bigger plan to make him rich beyond his dreams, right after she arrived back from the Fourth of July hoedown in Barberry, and they found a frightened Donny Charlton hiding under the tarp in the rear of the buckboard.

'Who the hell's this? Where's Sammy?' Winston grabbed young Donny by his shirt and shook him, glaring at Mattie.

'I didn't know he was there, Winston! I swear!'

'Where the hell is Sammy?'

'I – I couldn't find him,' she explained, voice trembling. 'You know what he's like, always running off and hiding. I – I couldn't find Donny here, neither, to ask where Sam was. I thought they'd both run off together. You know Sam always comes back after a few days. . . .'

Winston shook Donny. 'What're you doin' here, boy? Where's Sam?'

'They – they kidnapped, him. They thought he was me.'

Mattie and Winston stared, Mattie gasping.

'Two men – they jumped us, said they had some sky rockets for us. But one grabbed Sam and t'other dragged me off and cuffed me hard – said I was to keep my mouth shut or some night he'd come an' slit my throat. He showed me his knife an' everything. He thought I was Sammy. I was scared and hid under the tarp in your buckboard, but I din' know it was yours, Mrs Bale, honest Injun. . . .'

'That's all right, Donny, it's all right. But what've they done with my Sammy?'

'I – I heard 'em say whoever they worked for was

131

gonna ask for a big ransom, ten or twenty thousand dollars. Said Linus would pay it for me, that he'd be able to raise the money easy, him being with the bank.'

Winston leaned down quickly, holding Donny's shoulder hard so that the boy squirmed. 'Twenty thousand! For the likes of you! I don't believe it!'

'It's true!' Donny was upset now, tears brimming in hsi eyes. 'I – I want to go home to my ma. Those men scared me. . . .'

'That's all right, Donny. I'll drive you home. But we'll have some food first and—'

'The kid stays here,' Winston cut in, smiling crookedly, holding the boy's arm in a crushing grip. 'I mean, he's what you call a valuable asset, ain't you, kid? I bet they don't care who they pay that ransom to, long as they get you back safe and sound. Hell, I ain't greedy! I'll even settle for a nice big fat re-ward for keepin' this young man safe. 'Course it might be a few days before I let 'em know we've got him. By then, they'll be glad to pay just about anythin' I ask!'

He winked at the shocked, white-faced Mattie.

'Now, don't say your brother-in-law ain't got a brain or two in his head, eh?'

'Does your brain tell you what happens to Sam when they find out he's not the one they thought?' Her voice trembled and she began to shake. 'They'll probably kill him so he can't identify them!'

Winston composed his face. 'Don't reckon they will. Anyway, this one stays put. I ain't gonna let him outta my sight till I decide to tell that banker where I got him – an' how much it's gonna cost to get him back!'

CHAPTER 13

THE RANSOM

Red Carlin looked smug when they found the tracks some distance from the entrance to the snakelike canyon. They pointed towards the distant Bale farm, a long journey through the hills and the plains beyond.

'Reckon the kid was young Sam Bale after all.'

Smoky sucked down a sharp breath; he couldn't believe Red could be so loco as to rub Quinlan's nose in it this way.

The big man, squatting beside the tracks left by Cole, looked up bleakly, scratching idly at his short beard.

'Could be. Or Cole's got some idea of hiding the Charlton kid out there. Either way, we follow. And we do it without a lot of stupid talk.' He set his glare on Red, who swallowed and nodded, running the tip of his tongue around his thin lips.

'Whatever you say, Quick. I wouldn't put it past that damn sheriff to try to hide Donny Charlton.'

Quinlan straightened, hitched up the gun belt

around his thick waist.

'Kid don't matter – to hell with him, whoever he is. I want Cole – we've got some squarin' away to do. But better'n that, he still has the ransom money. *That*'s what counts now.'

Both Red and Smoky Hill nodded gently; for a while there they had forgotten that the whole point of this was to collect the money, had been too busy trying to decide the identity of the kid.

Now, like Quinlan said, that didn't matter: it was the cash that counted.

The cash and Cole, Red corrected himself.

He sure as hell wouldn't want to be in that sheriff's shoes when Quinlan should finally catch up with him.

Sam Bale was riding up behind Cole on the big black. It was so wide in the body that his short legs were stretched out and he squirmed around a lot in discomfort.

'Stay still,' Cole said shortly.

'I feel like I'm doin' the splits. My belly an' legs're nearly in a straight line, this blamed jackass is so darn wide!'

Cole reined up and Sam slid off gratefully, rubbing his groins and hips, stamping his feet.

'That feels good. Think I might run alongside for a spell.'

'With your legs we'll be going backwards. C'mon, sit in front of me. I'll slide back a bit in the saddle.'

It was better but Sam held the saddle horn, pushing against it constantly to keep it from pressing into his belly. 'I'm gonna be dead before we get home!'

'You keep up that bitchin' and you might be. You been playing too long with Donny Charlton. Linus reckons he's always complaining about something.'

'Yeah, well maybe he has cause to, way Linus treats him.'

'The considered opinion of an eight-year-old, eh? They just don't get along, is all. Like you and me won't, you keep bellyaching. You think riding like this is worse than being in that cave?'

Sam went quiet. They covered another mile before he said in a quieter tone, 'I was scared they was gonna kill me.'

'Understandable. They seemed mean types.'

'*They* was scared of someone called Quinlan. Boy, he sure had that Rooster and Blackie buffaloed. Kept checkin' my ropes, one or t'other, sayin' to make *blamed* sure I couldn't get away or Quinlan'd kill 'em both.'

'Guess he wanted it to go off just right, seeing as the kidnapping was his idea in the first place.'

Sam twisted a little and craned his neck to look up into Cole's dusty face.

'What gave you that notion?'

Cole tensed, frowning. After a few moments he said, 'Well, maybe he had some help from Brack Devlin. You know who he is?'

'I've heard of him. But no one mentioned his name while they had me.'

'Then why d'you doubt it was Quinlan's idea?'

'Just somethin' they said.'

'Which was?'

'Hey! Lookit! There's the farm!' Sam started squirming, throwing his short legs over the saddle horn and dropping off the black. 'Never thought I'd be so glad to see it!'

'Come back here! It's a couple of miles yet over those hills . . . Sam! Ah, dammit!'

He set the black after the boy who ploughed into thick brush, dodging about so the black couldn't follow without Cole having to keep a tight rein, trying to find a clear passage. The boy being so small, he could crawl under the bushes and it was hard to see just where he was.

The little tyke had decided to have some fun, dammit!

Cole was still fighting the black – the horse not happy at being constantly scratched up by the stiff, prodding brush – when the laughing kid burst out way ahead and scooted up the slope like a young, gangling deer.

Swearing at being outwitted by an eight-year-old, Cole forgot the livery man's admonition about spurs.

He touched them to the black's flanks, aiming on driving it through the dense brush in as straight a line as possible.

Bam! The world seemed to explode around him. The black whickered and half-reared, then snorted, swung its head and bit his lower leg. Even with the leather of the half-boot between his flesh and those big teeth, it hurt like the devil. Cole yelled, automatically leaned down to rub his lower leg.

The black plunged away and the brush raked across Cole's shoulders, swept him from the saddle. Spiky brush tore at his clothes, ripped a line of red across one cheek, caught under his six-gun butt, flicking it from the holster.

Cole dived after it and by the time he recovered the Colt and stood up, angrily freeing his loose shirt from snagging brush, the horse was through and running free, mane and tail flying.

Above, on top of the hill, he heard the full-blooded chortling amusement of the boy, who waved cheekily.

'Hope you catch him – eventually!'

Then he turned and disappeared over the crest of the hill, just an echo of his tinkling laughter reaching the angry sheriff.

Mattie Bale felt the hard ground against her knees as she worked in the vegetable garden, some twenty yards away from the cabin. She grabbed a handful of her old skirt, bunching the cloth so it made a pad beneath her sore knees.

At the same time she lifted her head. Her face was shaded by her straw hat as she looked towards the entrance to the root cellar just past the south end of the garden.

She thought she heard Donny Charlton again. Her heart started to beat faster, and she flicked her gaze towards the house, but there was no sign of Winston. Which didn't mean he wasn't watching from behind the curtain in the window of the bedroom.

It wasn't right, keeping Donny here! Especially locked away in the root cellar. But Winston Bale had his mind set on claiming the ransom for himself, or at least a substantial reward in exchange for Donny.

She had thought of trying to sneak out at night to release the boy, but Winston locked the bedroom door and kept the key on a thong around his neck.

And he always had an arm thrown across her body so that she only had to stir or turn over and he was instantly awake.

Funny! That cry wasn't coming from the root cellar – it was much clearer than Donny's muffled calls.

She heard it again and straightened, standing up completely now, turning to look at the low hogback rise. Her breath caught in the back of her throat as she glimpsed the small figure hurtling down the slope, tow hair wild, waving,the piping voice calling her name.

'Oh, dear God! Thank you, thank you!' She waved and hiked up her skirts, starting to run towards Sammy as his short legs pumped frantically in his excitement and pleasure at being home again.

Then she came to an abrupt halt, panting, alarmed to see a rider on a big black horse coming over the crest. He bore down on the running boy who looked wildly over his shoulder. The rider leaned down, fisted up a handful of Sammy's jacket and lifted him bodily, depositing the boy in front of him on the horse.

She put a hand to her mouth, screaming for Winston – of *all people*! But the rider continued on at a more sedate pace, rode into the yard and dropped Sammy to the ground only a few yards away.

The boy ran to his mother, who picked him up and was almost choked by the thin arms clamping around her head and neck. She felt her heart melt, the sting of tears.

'My! I haven't had *that* big a welcome for years!'

'Get down from that hoss, mister! And careful!'

Winston came around a corner of the cabin, holding a rifle, covering Cole, paying no attention to Sammy or the woman. The sheriff dismounted slowly, watching Winston closely.

'Who the hell's this?' Bale demanded.

'That's Sheriff Cole from Barberry,' Mattie told her brother-in-law. 'We've never met, but I know him by sight.'

Cole touched a hand to his hatbrim. 'Pleased to meet you, ma'am. You don't need that rifle, mister.'

'I'll decide that.'

'For heaven's sake, Winston! He's a *lawman*!'

'The sheriff rescued me from the kidnappers, Ma. Shot 'em both. *Wow!* Is he fast!'

Winston suddenly looked uncertain and the rifle barrel sagged. 'You ain't gonna harm the boy?'

Cole flicked his bleak gaze across the man and settled it on Mattie. 'Your boy was kidnapped in mistake for Donny Charlton, ma'am. . . .'

'Oh, yes, I know. Donny told us. . . .'

'Shut up, Mattie!'

But it was too late and Cole studied Winston as the woman explained how Donny had turned up here, some days ago, terrified the kidnappers were going to come after him.

'Where is he now?'

Mattie glanced at Winston who forced a weak smile. 'Well, the kid's so scared I put him in the root cellar. Convinced him he'd be safe there, no one could harm him.'

'How long's he been in there?'

'We-ell—'

'Ever since he arrived!' Mattie said quickly, cutting in over Winston's halting explanation; she saw how she could finally get rid of the man and his threat to her and Sam. 'Winston has some idea he'll hold him, and collect the ransom himself!'

'Damn you, woman!'

Winston brought up the rifle quickly but there was a gunshot and the weapon was smashed from his hands. He jumped back, hands tingling, looking at the splintered rifle stock on the ground at his feet.

Mattie cringed, hugging Sam tightly to her, staring wide-eyed at the smoking Colt in the sheriff's hand. He started forward and Winston, half-crouching, backed away.

'Listen. I din' mean no harm! It – it just seemed that if someone was willin' to pay for the kid's return—'

Cole hit him in the mouth, a backhanded blow from the left. Winston staggered and dropped to one knee.

'Sam, you go let Donny out.' Cole, keeping an eye on Winston, fumbled open one saddlebag on the sweating black and took out a set of manacles.

Winston was on his feet when Cole walked up to him and told him to hold out his hands.

'What the hell're you doin'? Aagh! Judas, they're too tight! You've pinched my skin!'

'You're lucky I don't break your jaw! What kind of snake are you, locking up a kid scared out of his wits in a dark cellar!' Cole shoved Winston roughly. 'Get over there and sit under that tree. You move and I'll shoot you in the leg.'

'Wh – what you gonna do with me?'

'Take you back to Barberry and up before Judge Cannon. He's got a grandson about Donny Charlton's age. I reckon you'll be either working on the chain gang or spending the next couple of years in the territorial pen.'

'What? For keepin' a kid safe in a root cellar?'

'Sammy told me about you taking over this farm and aiming to sell it out from under Miz Bale. And I got a good memory for faces. Yours is on a dodger from Creek County, in connection with a Wells Fargo robbery. "Winn Bailey". Know that name?'

Winston's shoulders slumped. Mattie frowned.

'Is that true, Sheriff? That he's a wanted man?'

'Yes, ma'am. I reckon he was hiding out here on your farm, it being so isolated. Saw a chance to make himself some easy money.'

Mattie walked across and slapped Winston's face. 'I don't see how you can possibly be Steven's brother! He was a fine man—'

'Yeah, yeah – and a poor one,' Winston said, surly now. ' "Honest Steve" we used to call him at Wells Fargo. Needed some extra money so's he could marry you, make an honest woman of you, and took a job as shotgun guard. Only he picked a stage that was held up and like the fool he was, died tryin' to stop the robbers. When I ran into a little trouble myself an' we had to scatter I recollected him talkin' about you and this farm he was buyin'. . . .'

Mattie, fighting back tears, looked as if she would

like to spit upon him. Then Sammy came running back with a filthy-looking Donny Charlton. The boy was blinking in the sunlight.

'Oh, you poor soul! Come on up to the house and I'll give you a good wash. Sam's clothes should fit you. . . .'

She led the subdued Donny towards the cabin. Sam started after her but Cole called him back.

'Sam. You were going to tell me something when you got all excited about seeing your farm and ran off.'

The boy blinked up at the tall sheriff. 'I wasn't gonna tell you anythin'.'

'You were talking about Rooster or Blackie saying something about who set up Donny Charlton's kidnapping.'

'Aw, yeah.' Sam glanced towards the cabin where his mother and Donny had now disappeared. 'Er – maybe I got it wrong. Might be better I don't say nothin' an' get someone into trouble.'

Cole leaned down, making his face stern. 'How about *you* being the one to get into trouble by *not* telling me?'

The sheriff flicked his gaze towards the sullen Winston in manacles slumped under the tree. Sam drew down a sharp breath.

'We-ell. They was talkin' about the ransom and how much it was, twenty thousand. Blackie said he couldn't imagine bein' so rich, that someone could lose that much gamblin'. And Rooster said, well, he reckoned it was a right smart idea of the banker's to have his own stepson kidnapped and then pay off his gamblin' debts

142

with a ransom put up by the kid's mother—'

' "The banker"? Linus Charlton?'

Sammy Bale shrugged. 'Guess so. Dunno who else they could mean.'

'No,' Cole said slowly. 'Me neither.'

CHAPTER 14

ALL SQUARED AWAY

Cole knew Quinlan and his men would be coming after him and Sammy Bale.

'Miz Bale. . . .'

'Mattie, please, Sheriff.'

He nodded. 'I answer best to just "Cole". Mattie, there are some men after me. The ones who kidnapped Sam. I reckon they'll be here soon and I don't want you left to face 'em. The leader's a miserable snake, goes by the name of Quinlan, and if he finds he's missed me here, he's likely to get real mad, might even burn the farm.'

'Oh, no!' Her hand went to her throat.

'It's possible, so I figure you and the boys, and Winston, better come with me to Barberry.'

'What if we meet this Quinlan along the way?'

'There'll be a fight. I won't lie to you. But it'll be best

out in the open.'

Her teeth tugged at her bottom lip and then she nodeed. 'All right. If you can hitch up the buckboard, I'll get ready and find some decent clothes for Donny to wear. I suppose I should try to repair his jacket, too. I don't know Mrs Charlton, but I hear she's kind of – finicky.'

He smiled. 'That's one word for it.'

Winston was still manacled under the tree and he watched as Cole prepared the buckboard.

'I can ride if you put my hands in front.'

The sheriff merely looked at him, finished harnessing the team.

'I won't try to escape. Give you my word.'

'You'll ride in the back of the buckboard,' Cole told him flatly.

And that was how they left the farm a short time later. Cole watched the backtrail frequently. Winston was stretched out on a tarp in the back of the buckboard, the boys riding up front with Mattie Bale who handled the team expertly.

Cole rode to high ground where he could, searching for sign of Quinlan, and it wasn't long before he saw a dust cloud that brought him standing up in the stirrups. It was coming in from the right direction, maybe slightly north, but by now Quinlan would have seen *their* dust and swung around to follow and check it out.

Cole rode back to the buckboard, coming up on the driving side. Mattie read his face, stiffened, and looked past him. She sucked in a sharp breath.

'Are those the men?'

' 'Fraid so, Mattie. We left it a mite late. The boys better get in the back, you too. You can handle the reins from the tray if you crouch down.'

'Yes, I've done it before.' At his quizzical glance she smiled. 'I grew up in Comanche country, in a sod hut. *Several* sod huts. We had to abandon them from time to time and twice I recall we had to outrun renegade bucks.'

'Don't want a job as deputy, do you?'

She laughed and slowed the team while the boys clambered into the back. Then she handed the reins to Sam while she followed. She knelt down, the reins running over the back of the driving seat now as she experimented to make sure she could give the signals to the team smoothly.

Winston huddled down lower; he was a man who always looked out for Number One. The boys were excited and just a little afraid. Neither wanted to show fear in front of the other, but their smiles were fixed.

Guns started banging. Just faint whipcracks at first, the bullets puffing dust well behind the buckboard. Cole unsheathed his Winchester but didn't return fire yet; he had no ammunition to waste.

Quinlan was unmistakable with his huge bulk, forking a big palomino, the rifle like a toy in his hands. Red Carlin rode a few yards to Quinlan's left, while Smoky Hill was at about the same distance to the right.

Cole could guess Quinlan's strategy: they would fire into the buckboard from the three different positions, likely trying for the team. Just downing one horse would be enough to wreck the buckboard – and, of course, they figured Cole would haul rein and ride back to help.

Then *he* would be the target for the three rifles.

So Cole angled away from the buckboard, trying to draw Quinlan's fire, but the big man made no attempt to go after him or even direct the guns towards the sheriff.

'You son of a bitch!' Cole murmured, swinging back towards the racing vehicle. 'Make targets out of women and kids!'

Quinlan knew Cole, knew the man wouldn't abandon the woman and boys, and also wouldn't want them harmed. Quinlan and his men were closing in on the vehicle now and splinters flew from the sides. Winston yelled. The boys lay flat, trying to press their small bodies into the rough planks. Mattie stretched out, driving more or less blindly now, but if she stayed on her knees, she would be too easy a target.

She guessed Quinlan would use her to draw Cole into his trap. There was little she could do about it, and she was worried the boys were in danger from the flying lead. Winston could take his chances, but the boys' safety concerned her.

Cole took the reins in his teeth, threw the rifle to his shoulder and quickly beaded Red Carlin, the closest rider. The gun jumped as he squeezed off his shot and a moment later, Red tumbled from the saddle.

In that brief passage of time Quinlan and Smoky Hill had closed in. Smoky was almost close enough now to leap from his saddle into the rear of the clattering, bouncing vehicle. He was poised to try and Cole, busy dodging bullets from Quinlan's rifle, couldn't get a bead on Hill. Then Sammy and Donny rose up and began throwing something at the killer. Smoky lifted his arms, dodging as well as he could, then three large potatoes and a cabbage hit him. He yelled as he tumbled out of the saddle. He bounced and screamed as he skidded in under the back wheels.

The buckboard bounced wildly and Mattie cried out as she was flung into Winston, almost losing her grip on the reins. He kicked at her but Sam had another cabbage in his fist now and slammed it down into Winston's face, screwing and pushing. The leaves tore loose, Winston started choking.

By then Mattie had control again.

Quinlan was too big and awkward to make the leap across but he bared his teeth, throwing a wild glance at the racing black with Cole lifting his rifle again, before aiming his own gun at the woman.

Cole drove home the spurs into the black's flanks.

In two mighty, whickering leaps the big horse smashed into Quinlan's palomino and both mounts went down, all a-tangle, throwing the riders.

Cole rolled maybe a dozen times, losing the rifle, digging in his boot heels in an attempt to slow his slide. Quinlan was rolling, too, but his large bulk didn't slide so far and he spun onto his side, teeth bared white against his jet-black beard, as he brought up his Colt.

He fired twice and stones leapt against Cole's face as he kicked away, spun and came up to one knee. Quinlan's six-gun swung around towards him, but it was Cole's Colt that blasted three fast shots. The lead knocked Quinlan flat but he tried to rise on his elbow, even though already choking on blood from a neck wound. He brought his gun up, holding it awkwardly in both his huge hands, eyes crazy and bulging with hate.

But the effort was just too much and he fell back, dead.

Linus Charlton knew something had gone wrong.

The ransom should have been paid over by now and young Donny returned. He didn't want any real harm to come to the boy but he couldn't help feeling pleased at the fright the kid would have had. He hoped Quinlan and the others hadn't been *too* tough with him.

But it was important that the ransom was paid over quickly – that was his masterstroke.

For weeks he had sweated and felt his ulcer burning holes in his stomach over the debt he owed Brack Devlin – via Mannering, curse his hide! If he had realized that Mannering at the Delta was part of Devlin's group he would never have turned a card or thrown a dice ... *No – he would have, just the same.* When the gambling fever gripped him, he would have bet his own mother's wedding ring if there was just that slim chance of his luck turning. . . .

He was lucky in one way, being president of the local bank, but in another it caused him more worry than he had ever known in his life before.

'We gave you all that credit, Linus, because you run the bank, you damn fool!' Mannering had told him.

As soon as the words were spoken, Linus felt sick and faint. 'The – the bank has nothing to do with it!'

'You think not? You think you have such a winnning personality – combined with a *losing streak* – that I would extend you all that credit? Wake up, Linus! You owe money, a lot of money, and you run the local bank. Doesn't that set ideas running around in that porridge you use for brains?'

He almost did faint then. 'No! It – it's ridiculous! I can't use the bank's money! It's – it's more than my job is worth.'

Mannering had looked at him bleakly. 'Wrong, Linus. It could be more than your *life* is worth.'

It was only a matter of time, of course. Pressure, relentless pressure – the threat of losing his house, his job, *Bess* – and he was driven into the hell of embezzlement.

Surprisingly, after the first time – and doing it successfully – it became easier. Twice more, and then the amount he had stolen from the bank reached 5,000 dollars.

He almost died of fright; it was such a large amount to account for that the first audit, due in a month or so, would pick it up almost immediately.

That was when Mannering informed him that he actually owed the money to Brack Devlin's group. A few days later Quick Quinlan arrived, and when he left Linus was nursing two broken fingers, with the promise that they were only the beginning.

They gave him a week to come up with the money, or find some way to get it. They were demanding 10,000 dollars! Some stupid talk about high expenses and interest on the principal. As if he couldn't see it was

150

straight-out robbery, with him cast as the robber!

But his life was worth more than 20,000 dollars, which was a combination of his gambling debt (15,000 by now) and what he had embezzled. And *that* money had to be paid back into the bank's records immediately!

Then, after yet another clash with that blasted kid, and Bess, as usual, taking Donny's side, Linus had the bitter thought: *I wish he'd have an accident – or someone would abduct the little swine. . . .*

That was when the magnificent idea had struck him, fully formed, no less!

Arrange a kidnapping, demand a ransom – enough to cover the gambling debt *and* the embezzled money – and all his worries would be over.

The biggest problem would be getting the ransom together. How could he do it? The bank might lend him the money because of his service and position, but there would be close scrutiny of his personal accounts and spending and . . . No, that was out; his embezzlement would soon be discovered.

If he forgot about approaching the bank, that only left Bess and her inheritance. But brother-in-law Carl was the problem there. Tight-fisted, dollar signs where his heart should be.

But, at who knew what cost to his health, he had eventually persuaded Bess to prevail upon Carl to allow her access to the trust fund. After all, Donny was Carl's nephew.

Devlin was agreeable, and that told Linus that the idea must have merit; Devlin was too smart to get

151

involved in anything that could easily go wrong.

He had it all worked out: get the money together, 20,000 dollars, which would allow him to pay off Devlin and put the embezzled money back. Then, write a series of ransom notes, and. . . .

But who would pay the money over? Not Linus! Oh, no, he couldn't get involved in that part, but there was Sheriff Cole! A friend, a man handy with a gun in case of unforeseen trouble. . . .

That was the answer and, thankfully, Cole had agreed to do the job. A tough man, but still a soft touch in some ways.

But why hadn't it worked? He was certain something must have gone wrong. There should have been word by now, and the boy should have been returned. He should have been notified and. . . .

With trembling hand, he reached for the whiskey bottle, surprised to see how little remained. *How many bottles did that make since this horror had started?* What did it matter? He drank it down straight from the neck, jumped when his office door opened and Sheriff Cole strode in, closing the door behind him.

One look at the lawman's face and Linus knew it was all over.

But he had to brazen it out; there was no other way, and anyway, while he protested his innocence, he might find a solution that would let him off the hook. After all, Cole was a friend, wasn't he, not just a lawman who went blindly by the book. . . ?

And he was a man of honour. Linus had played upon this trait, taken advantage of it, and he would again if he could just find a way to do it.

'What news, Cole?' he rasped, aware that his voice was shaky and that he still held the whiskey bottle by the neck. He gave a fleeting grin, waving the bottle. 'I – I've been worried sick, waiting to hear if everything's all right. It *is* all right, isn't it?'

Cole dropped into the chair opposite the desk, thumbed back his battered hat, hooked a boot over one leg and took out tobacco sack and papers. He began to make a cigarette.

'Donny's home safe with your wife, Linus.'

The banker sighed and his mouth twitched as a laugh of relief wanted to burst out of him. 'Oh, thank God! You don't know how much I appreciate what you've done for me, Cole. And Donny *is* safe and sound? They didn't – harm him?'

Cole shook his head. 'No, he's fine.'

'Good! I admit I don't like the boy very much, but I wouldn't've wished him any real harm.'

'But you took the risk just the same.' Cole cupped a hand around the match flame and glanced across at the banker as he lit the cigarette.

Linus looked grey, sitting stiffly in his chair, frowning now. 'I don't understand. *I* took the risk? What risk are you talking about?'

'You took the risk that Quinlan and the others wouldn't do Donny any real hurt while the ransom was gathered and paid over.'

Linus ran a tongue across dry lips and nodded slowly. 'Well . . . that couldn't be helped. I mean, I don't see how you can think I'm to blame in any way. I had no

153

choice. I was rawhided into finding the ransom money, which I did – as fast as possible. Yes, I suppose, in a way, I *did* take the risk of Donny getting rough treatment, but there was absolutely nothing I could do about it, Cole, you must see that.'

Cole exhaled smoke. 'There would have been no risk at all if you hadn't arranged Donny's kidnapping in the first place, Linus.'

The banker was very still now, eyes almost glazed as he stared unseeingly across his office. It seemed a long time before his gaze focused on Cole's sober face.

'I . . . don't believe I heard you aright, Cole. *I* arranged Donny's kidnapping?' He stood, outraged. 'In the name of God, what're you saying?'

'Sit down, Linus. It's all over now. Almost all over, I guess, is what I mean. It could've worked, but Devlin's men made a mistake. They didn't have a good description of Donny, and identified him by his tow-coloured hair, but mostly by the jacket he was wearing. Only he'd given it to Sammy Bale after he fell in the river.'

Linus, frowning and trying not to show the trembling that now possessed him, sat down slowly, staring.

'Are you saying . . . do you mean Sammy Bale was abducted istead of Donny?'

'That's it.'

Linus blinked. 'Well, what . . . The ransom . . . They wouldn't've known they had the wrong boy: They'd have believed they had Donny, just taken the ransom and. . . .'

His words faded slowly as Cole began to shake his head. Linus slumped.

'Tell me what happened,' he said with sudden resignation.

So Cole told him.

Tears squeezed from Linus Charlton's eyes and rolled down his fat cheeks – no longer pink and healthy looking, but now resembling the gaunt face found on a day-old corpse.

Cole smoked his cigarette down, thumbed it out in the metal ashtray on the desk.

The banker remained silent, looking down at his finger-locked hands in his lap. Slowly, his haunted eyes lifted to Cole's face and his voice seemed considerably steadier and stronger.

'You killed Quinlan?'

'A bullet was too quick for that son of a bitch, but, yeah, he's dead now. So are some others who worked for Devlin.'

'What about him?'

'I'll ride down and see him. I reckon there're a few charges I can hang on him.'

Linus scoffed. 'Not with the lawyers he'll hire.'

'Then I'll burn down his saloon . . . casino, or whatever he likes to call it.'

'You – you'd do that?'

'Not for you, Linus. But because it's time someone put a stop to Devlin, one way or another.'

'Yes – well, I believe you're probably the only man who could do it, Cole. I suppose Bess knows everything?'

'I didn't tell her.'

Linus smiled ruefully. 'That damn Donny will! Funny

thing is, I believe I'm more afraid of Bess than – the bank or even the law.'

'She did say she'd be going to California, and probably staying there.'

The banker almost laughed. 'And just how would she leave me? She's mighty vindictive, Cole. She'll leave my life in utter ruins before she goes, you mark my words. She'll have me humiliated, made a figure of fun and shame. . . .'

Cole realized that Linus was probably right and he felt a surge of sympathy for the banker.

'You've been a damn fool, Linus.'

The banker sighed, sat back and spread his hands. He looked at them; the trembling had stopped

'Yes, I have. And I only have myself to blame.'

Cole stood. 'I won't do you the indignity of putting the manacles on you, Linus, but I want you to come with me. Now.'

'Yes, of course.' He started to open a desk drawer, saying, 'I'll just get a few things and—'

Cole dropped a hand to his gun butt. 'Let's just go, Linus. Get your coat and hat and we'll stroll on down to the law office, just as we've done fifty times in the past. No one needs to know anything's wrong at this stage.'

'Thanks, Cole. You're – considerate.'

The banker went to a closet, put on his grey coat and took down his hat, setting it squarely on his head.

'Do I look my usual smug self?' he asked with a sad smile.

'You look OK.'

Cole held the office door open and Linus pushed past him, pausing to glance around at the clerks working at their desks and behind the counters. He nodded curtly to himself as Cole closed the door.

'One more favour, Cole. . . ?'

'Don't push it, Linus.'

The banker smiled. 'Wouldn't dream of it. Look, I know I have to face Bess. I've got just one shot of whiskey left in my desk bottle. Let me take that one more slug, and then I'll be ready to – to face the music.'

Cole studied his face soberly. Linus met his gaze and smiled faintly.

'For old times' sake, Cole. . . .'

A brief hesitation, then the sheriff nodded. 'OK. Don't take too long.'

'No. I won't keep you waiting. Promise.'

He opened the office door and went in quickly, closing the door after him.

Cole leaned his wide shoulders against the office wall, thinking of Bess Charlton and her utter vindictiveness.

What the hell did people, men or women, get out of making life so miserable for so many others? he wondered.

Through the wall, he heard a desk drawer open and, at the same time, remembered seeing the whiskey bottle on Linus's desk.

It had been empty!

He lunged for the door and had it part-way open when the pistol shot cracked against his ears.

He was just in time to see Linus falling forward across

157

his desk, the small, pearl-handled derringer dropping from his lifeless fingers.

Cole was behind his own desk, struggling to make out his report for the records, when there was a soft knock on the street door a moment before it opened.

Mattie Bale stepped inside, smiling, still dressed in her dusty clothes from the wild ride into Barberry.

'Am I interrupting?'

'Nothing I can't finish later.' Cole stood up and walked around the desk, offering her the visitor's chair. She smiled as she sat down and he went back around to his own chair. He nodded to the window.

'Getting on for sundown. You'll be driving in the dark.'

'I've decided to stay over in town tonight. Sammy will enjoy it. He's playing with Donny Charlton at the livery just now. Well, not playing, more like working. Earl's promised them two bits each if they fork some hay for him. I suspect they'll only be moving it from one place to another. But he likes kids, does Earl.'

'Yeah – a real family man.'

'Forgive me if I'm prying, Sheriff, but you seem to me like you'd make a good . . . family man.'

He met her steady gaze. 'Once, maybe.' Then without conscious volition, he added, 'There was a fire. My wife and son – didn't get out in time.'

She reached across the desk and her small hand squeezed his – a spontaneous gesture of sympathy.

'I'm sorry if I stirred . . . bad memories.'

He smiled. 'No bad memories. I just think about the

good times, and the good times that might've been.'

She nodded slowly. 'Well, that's a fine way to handle such a tragedy.'

'I've only just managed to figure it out. For a long time there I – I lived too much in the past.'

'I'm glad things are better for you now, then. I want to thank you for saving Sam. It was very brave.'

'Wish I'd got there sooner.'

'I'm very grateful. What'll happen to Winston?'

'He's in the cells with another man named Creed. They'll both be facing the judge in a few days.'

She nodded a little absently, tapping work-worn fingers against the edge of his desk. 'I didn't really come to ask about Winston,' she confessed and his smile grew wider. 'Oh! You knew! I must be more transparent than I thought.'

'Well, I figure you for a good woman, Mattie, but I don't see you as worrying too much about Winston's welfare.'

She laughed briefly. 'No. He deserves some time in jail. What I really came for was to ask you . . . if you're ever out our way, near the farm, that is, why don't you stop by and I'll cook you a meal? I mean, being a bachelor, you must grow tired of buying indifferent food and—'

'Sure. That's a good idea. I'll be coming by to get your statement in a day or so. . . .'

'I could give it to you now. Oh! Yes, yes do that, Cole. Try to make it about lunchtime.'

He stood and reached down his hat from the wall peg. 'All this talk about food's making me hungry. How about I buy you supper at Farrel's diner? They do a good pot-roast on a Thursday night. . . .'

'This is Friday.'

'They serve it cold on Fridays, with a fresh salad. Mighty good on the palate, so they say. Sometimes even have ice cream for later.'

She laughed and took the arm he offered her as they made for the office door.

'I think we'd better check it out, don't you?'

'Best idea I've heard today. C'mon.'